AF656045

URBAN SOCIAL STRUCTURE
A STUDY OF A HILL CITY

URBAN SOCIAL STRUCTURE
A STUDY OF A HILL CITY

SUROJIT SEN GUPTA

AKANSHA PUBLISHING HOUSE
NEW DELHI-110002

AKANSHA PUBLISHING HOUSE
4649-B/21, Ansari Road
Darya Ganj, New Delhi - 110 002
Email: ektabooks@yahoo.com
Ph.: 23263193/9811582579

Urban Social Structure : A Study of a Hill City

© Author

First Published 2006
ISBN 81-8370-050-0

All rights reserved. No part of this publication may be reproduced or transmitted, in any form or by any means, without prior permission of the author.

Any person who does any unauthorized act in relation to this publication may be liable to criminal prosecution and civil claims for damages.

[The responsibility for the facts stated, conclusions reached etc. is entirely that of the Authors. The publisher is not responsible for them, whatsoever.]

PRINTED IN INDIA

Published by M.P. Misra for Akansha Publishing House, New Delhi and Printed at Tarun Offset Press, Delhi

Dedicated To

My Mother, *Smti. Bani Sen Gupta* who has always been a part of inspiration and encouragement for all my academic endeavours.

CONTENTS

ACKNOWLEDGEMENT

I express my deep debt of gratitude to my supervisor Prof. A. C. Sinha of the Department of Sociology, North Eastern Hill University for his inspiration, guidance and assistance which he provided me in every step of my research work. I would also like to thank Prof. P. M. Chacko, Head of the Department of Sociology, North Eastern Hill University, for his valuable help and cooperation. I will be falling in my duty if I do not thank all my teachers for their support. Special thanks are also due for help received from Prof. Imdad Hussain, Department of History, Prof. A.C. Mahapatra, Department of Geography and Dr. Gurudas Das, Department of Economics, North-Eastern Hill University, Shillong.

My sincere thanks to the Indian Council of Social Science Research (NERC) for giving me the opportunity to visit Osmania University, Hyderabad under the study scheme grant. I would also like to thank Mr. Gideon Kharkongor Lecturer, Geography Department, St. Edmund's College, Shillong for his outstretched hands in drawing out the required maps in this research study.

My special thanks go to Mr. Tosan Kharsati for helping me in collecting data from the field. Thanks are due to Mr. Surajit Chakraborty for helping me in statistical work and to Mr. Tapan Dhar who extended all the possible help from time to time for completing this work. I am grateful to the authorities of Urban Affairs Department, Census Department, and Municipal Department, Government of Meghalaya for helping me with available information from time to time.

I am extremely thankful to my loving parents for standing by me through the period of my tension and stress with endurance and cheerfulness. I also wish to express my love and indebtedness to my dear brother and sister who were a constant source of support and inspiration and affection throughout the period of my struggle. I also wish to express my heartful thanks to my friends and relatives for continuously and constantly encouraging me to carry on the task I had undertaken.

Thanks are also recorded in favour of all those who positively responded to my Questionnaire schedule—too many to be named—who have in many ways helped me in enriching my work. My indebtedness lies also to the staff members of various libraries and institutions for providing me the timely access to the research material therein.

I express my gratitude to Dr. U. Sewa, of the Department of English, North Eastern Hill University, Shillong who was kind enough to read the draft. Last, but not the least, I would like to extend my sincere thanks and gratitude to Mr. Ksan K. Kharshiing, who without hesitation, and within a very short period of time amidst his busy schedules was able to print this research to the best of his ability.

Surojit Sen Gupta

LIST OF TABLE

LIST OF MAP

LIST OF FIGURE

1

INTRODUCTION

The chapter introduces the theme of the study under different heads. It reviews the various Theories on Urbanization, surveys, the urban scenario in the country in general and North East India in particular. At the end it reports on the strategy and method of the study.

UNDERSTANDING THE URBAN PHENOMENA

The urban centre is a place where the concentration of population takes place with marked secondary and tertiary occupations, having a municipality and notified area committee. Urbanism, on the other hand, is a social behaviour in urban areas, e.g., there is a marked differentiation in social structure as the people of diverse areas live close together. In urban areas one person meets with thousand persons in a day and hence it may not be possible for an urbanite to remember all of them for a longer period. Thus, urbanization, on the other hand, is a process of social transformation from rural to urban areas. In this sense, one place may be more urbanized in comparison with the other whether the same may be a village or town. A certain percentage of people in urban areas are found to be engaged in cultural activities and similarly the urban component of secondary and tertiary populations are found in villages. In this way, the urbanization of one place is a comparative feature which may continue or decline or even stop or is found in lesser degree; or there may be a high level of urbanization.

It is quite evident that due to the increasing urbanization the merger of villages into towns has been observed. Due to this process, the small towns develop into major urban centres. This also helps in transforming rural way of life into urban economic and social organization. The transformation of rural service centres is in both time and space, due to concentration of commercial, transportation, and professional services, give rise to the development of urban centres. The increasing intensity of such processes over a landscape leads to urbanization. The growth of urban centres also leads to changes in infrastructure, which in turn further affect regional development, industrialization, transportation linkages, population distribution, and the entire rural-urban continuum. At the same time, the dynamics of regional economics, population growth, increasing employment in the tertiary sector, and the continuation of these processes for longer period of time and over increasing dimensions of space, are signs of regional development. Thus urbanization is a polarization technique, which has been adopted for regional development.

Urbanization usually brings with it regional prosperity, as the provision of infrastructure facilities stimulate the development of locally available resources, increasing regional income and employment levels. Hence urbanization and regional development are closely correlated and cannot be separated. However, exceptions to the general pattern of regional prosperity abound. Urban slums, for example, are areas of regional, economic, cultural, political and social deprivation; they have not reaped the rewards of urbanization and regional development.

The dynamics of urbanization, however, is complex one. The natural increase of the existing urban population adds to the total number of people from adjoining regions and tends to concentrate to already crowded clusters, on the other. The concentration of population in such clusters is guided both by push factors in the adjoining regions and pull factors operating in the urban centres. The factors pushing population away from the rural areas towards the urban centres may vary in their significance from the one region to the other or from one country to the other. These factors may embrace in them (a) high growth of rural population due to high birth rate; (b) reduction in the need of agricultural labours due to improved agricultural technology; (c) increasing demand for items other than food-stuff due to increase in income; and (d) relatively low and uncertain returns from farm products. The relative strength of each push factor, however, varies with different geographic situations, such as (a) is more important in developing countries and (b) more in highly developed countries (Hagget, p. 1983).

The growth of an urban centre, on the other hand, is directly proportional to the strength of pull factors operating within its area. The pull factors may broadly be categorized under two major heads: (i) Agglomeration economies of the towns; and (ii) Urban multipliers. Agglomeration economies refer to the economic development set in motion by high density crowding and cumulative and cyclical growth of economies caused by serving an increasingly large market distributed over a small and compact geographic area. Consequently, the profits, owing to lowering of cost per unit resultant upon large production of articles and lower transportation costs in serving the local city market, increases. In addition, profit is also made by utilizing the machine and specialized knowledge of labours to the full. As specialization increases the dependence of one specialized branch on the other increases leading to sectorisation of the settlement making room for new arrivals that must follow. This led Lampard to the view that 'city growth is simply the concentration of differentiated but functionally integrated specialisms' (Lampard, 1965).

Urban multipliers may broadly be studied under two sub-heads of basic and non-basic activities of the towns. Basic activities as Hagget (Hagget, p. 1983) suggests refer to the activities that let the town sell goods or services or investments beyond their immediate boundaries. In the process expand the economic base of the towns to enable them to absorb more people from adjoining regions. Basic activities, thus, are essentially associated with the manufacturing industries. This also is the basis of 'urban base ratio', i.e. the ratio between the number of jobs in basic activities, and the total population. Non basic activities, on the other hand, refer to the activities the product of which is consumed in the town itself. The expansion of non-basic activities is positively proportionate to that of basic activities and population (Lowry model). Basic and non-basic economic activities and their expansion are the major multipliers to the urban population hence the urban growth.

Degree of urbanization in a region does provide a fair measure of its social and economic progress. Urban development, as the historical evidences suggest, takes place as a consequence of structural transformation of the economy from subsistent peasant based production to a surplus generating economy wherein a substantial segment of the working population gets engaged in non-agricultural pursuits. The functional quality of towns gets closely associated with the stage of socio-economic development. The geographic patterning of urbanization, therefore, is seen as a vital clue of socio-economic transformation in any region. Urbanization unlike many other socio-economic phenomena presupposes ever-increasing interactions over time and space in its intensity and dimensions. Thus, nature, modes, terms and stages of interactions play an important role in the processes and nature of urbanization. Urbanization also presupposes socio-economic and spatial differentiation; therefore, the study of urbanization need not be and should not be done by using the concepts which are valid for the analysis of undifferentiated phenomena. Therefore, it is imperative to change the terrain and the conceptual tools of analysis for a meaningful study of the issue of urbanization.

Urbanization is always and everywhere a consequence of structural changes in the economy, polity and the spatial components of a region/society. Therefore, it is not only conceptually fallacious but also a historical to maintain urbanization is the cause of bringing about structural change as is the case with many scholars. Urbanization presuopposes and thrives on perpetuating spatial and sectoral dependencies; therefore it is always antithetical to development and regional balance. The structure and functions of an urban area in its first and the last instance represent the nature of organic linkages between the urban centre and its hinterland both within and without.

Urbanization in the underdeveloped world has always been an episode of discontinuity and rupture from its heritage and traditional past. Most often it is experienced that urbanization in these countries shows a jumbled up of things and aspects highly uncorrelated to each other, i.e. incompatibility between the socio-economic formation and the superstructure or between the economic organization and the market relations etc. The processes of urbanization in the context of an omnipresent modern world system is directly related to the expansion and consolidation of the forces of the world market. Therefore, urbanization in the present context implies the drain of resources and economic surplus from the less advantageous regions to the advantageous ones.

It is a common knowledge that urbanization tends to occur more speedily when countries are in early stages of industrialization. A steady increase in its degree of urbanization is just natural. Now, with urbanization proceeding at a rapid speed, there is an increasing need for urban research, not only for understanding the growth trends and the factors involved therein but also for finding a solution to the urban problems created by the rising tide of urbanization.

Urban Processes

Various scholars have conceptualized urbanization in terms of the demographic aspect of city growth. For example, Kingsley Davis (Davis, et.al, 1962) has observed that urbanization depends upon the proportion of the total population concentrated in urban settlements or else to a rise in this proportion. A population within a given territory may redistribute itself through either centripetal or centrifugal movement. Centripetal movement is the process by which population and resources are drawn into a centre of population concentration- relatively larger numbers and higher density in a given area. Centrifugal movement is the process by which populations and resources move outward toward the periphery of a centre and further develop relations with a hinterland. The major process of centripetal movement is urbanization. Thus understood, urbanization may be viewed as the process of population concentration in which the ratio of urban people to the total population in a territory increases. From this point of view, an increase in both the size of individual urban concentration and the number of points of urban concentration may occur without an increase in urbanization of a territory, although these changes usually are accompanied by a rising proportion of population living in cities. Thus, seen, we may say that urbanization occurs only when a large proportion of inhabitants come to live in cities.

From the existing literature on urbanization, Paul. K. Hatt and Albert. J. Reiss Jr. (Hatt and Reiss, 1957) conclude that five major factors stand out as determinants of city growth and urbanization, of which the 'demographic revolution' is an important factor. Hope Tisdale (Tisdale, 1942) also calls attention to the demographic underpinnings of the city. Neither it's power and influence over the surrounding hinterland nor it's cosmopolitan culture can satisfactorily identify the city, because each of these, in fact, presupposes that urbanization has already taken place. Thus, according to him, population concentration alone is the essential condition of urbanism and urbanization. The development of a dense aggregation of people is necessary if any of the other properties of the city is to be observed. As a result, Tisdale acknowledges that the advancement of technology is an indispensable basis for the concentration of population without which the urban condition is a literal impossibility.

The advancement of technology is connected with the process of industrialization. If we accept Tisdale's view, it will mean that industrialization is a precondition of urbanization. And it is no wonder that the good many sociologists have considered industrialization and urbanization together. For example, Leonard Reissman (Reissman, 1964), observes, "Nowhere has industrialization ... occurred without urban development," and he warns us of the dangers of urbanization preceding industrialization.

Radhakamal Mukerjee (Mukerjee, R., 1940), emphasised the point that the process of urbanization is neither necessarily correlated with the process of industrialization nor both these processes are synonymous of each other. It is quite possible that the process of urbanization might have accelerated to a great extent without even the advent of industrialization. He suggests that both these processes should be understood as independent of each other, having different meanings.

One approach regards urbanization as a process of radiation, whereby ideas and practices spread out from the urban centre into surrounding areas. But Hope Tisdale rejects this approach on the ground that it makes the city the cause of urbanization rather than the result or the product of urbanization. Nor does it explain the appearance and growth of cities. It points the pre-existence of cities.

The process of urbanization has also been viewed by some as the increase in the intensity of problems or traits or characteristics that are essentially urban. Such a view may be criticized on the ground that it confuses cause and effect, the presupposition of cities before urbanization. In its logical analysis such an approach would mean that as problems are solved, as traits disappear, as characteristics change, deurbanization sets in. In modern times we observe many urban trends. We can easily refuse to call their intensification urbanization until we are sure that the growth of cities cannot proceed without their intensification, and also that the traits cannot intensify without a concomitant urban increase.

The process of urbanization must culminate in the city, if it is to be the process which makes the city. Thus viewed, just as long as cities grow in size, urbanization is taking place. It can stop, recede or go on at any point in time and space. There can be urbanization at one time and not at another. Thus, urbanization process as a continuous ongoing process has been wrongly assumed by various scholars. There can be rapid urbanization and slow urbanization; there can be deurbanization. There can be urbanization before there are cities and after there have been cities. Besides, it is also true that there can be absence of urbanization even though there may be many cities.

So far as the density of population as criterion of urbanization is concerned, some scholars have raised serious objections. For example, Gerald Breese (Breese, G., 1969), points out that it is not feasible to relate the degree of urbanization of a country to its overall density of population, as it is quite possible to have a relatively high level of urbanization and still have a low density of population for the country as a whole, example, Argentina. However, according to him, the relationship between the degree of National urbanization and energy consumption appears to be a useful index: the countries most urbanized are generally those with high energy consumption rates.

Olof Boustedt along with G. Goudswaard, develops the concept of "agglomeration area" to describe the process of urbanization. They use three important criteria to determine the urbanization process: residential pattern, economic structure and employment-residence ratio. For the same agglomeration concept, Prof. P. Geddes uses the term "Conurbation" (Geddes, 1968). But the entire process of urbanization all over the world has not been through conurbation. William H. Ludlow, Jack P. Gibbs, Donald J. Bogue and Emerson Seim, and Harley L. Browning have sought to lay definitive characteristics of urbanization, such as population size, density areas, extent and spatial shape, instead of solely depending on any one of these. J. P. Gibbs finds a logical connection among these attributes (Gibbs, J. P. 1966).

Edward B. Olds, Calvin F. Schmid, William H. and Jack P. Gibbs believe that the urbanization process be understood in terms of spatial structure. According to them, the study of urban spatial structure deals with a wide range of topics which encompasses patterns in the location of such diverse phenomena as places of residence, commercial establishments, transportation lines, ethnic groups, places of worship, manufacturing plants, vacant land, hospitals, public parks and areas demarcated along social class lines.

F. H. W. Green, Howard L. Green, Leslie Kish, John M. Mattila and Wilbur R. Thompson, L. L. Pownall, Howard J. Nelson, and Walter Isard and Robert Kavesh (as quoted by Sarlkwal, 1978) have described the urbanization process in terms of the development of urban hinterland and functional centres. They point out that the development of urban service areas, metropolitan regions and functional types are relevant to an explanation of the existence of urban places and to understand differences among them with regard to the characteristics generally attributed to such places.

James A. Quinn divides the characterization of urban growth into two categories: emergence of legal cities and of natural cities, the former as one kind of government unit, the latter as a natural social entity (Quinn, 1967). The legal city consists of a legally incorporated area (i.e., municipality) whose population exceeds a specific minimum and within whose boundaries a local government exercises authority as delegated by the state. The natural city constitutes a unit which can be marked off from neighbouring territory by such characteristics as size and density of population, typical occupations and quality of social relations. Quinn further observes three qualities of population other than density and size-mobility, permanence and heterogeneity-as are of possible value in characterizing urban areas, though none of them alone seems very useful.

Quinn also goes a little further and conceives of an urban area as something more than a large dense aggregation of people, buildings, and non-agricultural occupations, and as something different from an area characterized by complex, impersonal social relations. It may be viewed also as an internally organized community. He mentions two aspects of the internal organizations of an urban area-spatial and social. Spatially, an urban area contains several kinds of sub-areas: a central shopping district, secondary commercial areas of different sizes, wholesale areas, areas of light and heavy industries, and a considerable variety of residential areas. Each of these sub-areas has important relations with each other and is connected with others by lines of transportation and communications. Socially, the urban area includes a variety of institutions, classes and groups which, notwithstanding the high degree of segmentations of personal life, become organized bodies into an inclusive social unit and into a number of distinctive little social worlds. Generally, the institutions formed within an urban area become functionally integrated in such a manner that most residents obtain locally the satisfaction of their basic needs.

Gerald Breese finds that the characteristics of urbanization in newly developing countries are best understood in the context of the total changes in each growing country (Breese, 1969). For example, the nature and extent of urbanization may be diverse in the case of those countries which have been under colonial rule because urbanization has taken place in the periods of colonization or exploitation by foreign countries, or in connection with the emergence of nationhood following the end of colonial experience. There may also be urbanization of considerable magnitude even prior to colonial period. The urbanization of certain countries also reveals evidence of the conflicts which led to floods of refugees moving towards the large cities, and of the relationship of military key-points and supply centres to the development of the city.

Thus, the approaches so far discussed consider mostly the concentration of population as an essential factor of urbanization. Of course, there are many things about these concentrations which are different. There are ways of behaving, physical aspects, kinds of urbanization, types of activities which develop in and by virtue of the city. Some are different because they are in the city; some are in the city because they are different. But all these are not to be confused with the process of urbanization.

It is also significant that everything that affects population movement affects urbanization one way or the other. Most events are complex enough to have a bifurcated effect upon it. Thus, as Breese also held, it is the total effect of social change in a society upon population distribution that determines the course of urbanization.

But such a view of urbanization would further imply that togetherness of a progressive nature is an essential indicator of urbanization. It would also imply freeing of a part of the population from land and availability of greater labour force for more urban jobs. It would also imply progressive expansion of urban jobs. In this context, two conditions appear to be necessary for urbanization at an industrial centre. One is people and the other is technology. Population increase and surplus feed the process of urbanization, and technology and urbanization work together. In this case the density of population does not increase unless industries develop and technological advancement is made. Moreover, in this process the pace of urbanization also increases. But one thing is clear: development of technology does not depend upon the growth of population, rather the truth is just the reverse.

Apart from the approaches to the population concentration, there are other approaches to urbanization, which appear more germane to developing a proper perspective about it. Thus, on a realistic plane, urbanization is also understood as the process of becoming, i.e., a movement not necessarily direct or steady or continuous, from a state of non-urbanization towards a state of more concentration. It is put in motion by events or conditions which make concentration both possible and desirable. These events are not to be confused with the process itself. For example, the discovery and utilization of electricity constitute the series of events which have served to simulate urbanization. Similarly, the opening of large number of factories constitutes a series of events which attract a good deal of labour force from surrounding areas as also businessmen from distant areas and thus leading to concentration of population in a given territory. Still further, the development of transport and communication systems constitutes a series of events which stimulates urbanization. Various social distributions spontaneously spring up in a series of events which further simulate urbanization. Patterns of living may also occur in a series of events and simulate urbanization. As an exponent of this view, mention may be made of J. Clyde Mitchell who analyses the process of urbanization as "being the process of becoming urban, moving to cities, changing from agriculture to other pursuits common to cities and corresponding changing of behaviour patterns" (Mitchell, 1966).

Such an approach to urbanization may be disputed on the ground that the process of becoming is never perfect or complete; the moment it becomes static and assumes a certain fixed course it becomes a historical fact and remains no longer a process. Many migrants in the city live in it but they do not identify themselves with its accepted pattern of life. Thus, R.E. Pahl observes that many rural migrants are able to be in the city but not of it, using their more traditional 'rural' culture as a shock-absorber, or perhaps devising new transitional forms which are neither typically 'rural' nor typically 'urban'. He shows that the migrants reflect urban behaviour only during their working hours while outside they adhere to their rural behaviour patterns (Pahl, 1968). Mayer's observations in this regard are: "while some are born 'urban' and others achieve urbanization, none can be said to have urbanization thrust upon them". He terms this process of urbanization as 'incapsulation': the situation where migrants live in the city but are not urbanized (Mayer, 1974).

Urbanization is also understood in terms of the urban system in contrast to the non-urban system. Following this approach, the movement we say that a non-urban area has become urbanized, we immediately, rather unconsciously, refer to a social system characteristic of urban society. Such an urban system has been understood variously by different sociologists. For example, MacIver and Page (1959) designate such a system as having properties like heterogeneity, more agencies of social control, individualistic tendencies, cultural diversity etc. Louis Wirth describes these properties as heterogeneity, highest degree of dependence upon others, the segmental character of urban social relations and the sophistication and rationality of the inhabitants (Wirth, 1938). According to Louis Wirth, the central problem of the sociologists of the city is to discover the forms of social action and organizations that typically emerge in relatively permanent, compact settlements of large numbers of heterogeneous individuals. He further clarifies that, on the basis of the above three variables, it is possible to explain the characteristics of urban life and to account for the differences between cities of various sizes and types.

TRADITIONS OF URBAN STUDIES

Urban Ecology

Ecological approach focuses on the relationship between urban population and the habitat, as pioneered by Robert E. Park and Ernest W. Burgess and a team of scholars of Chicago University. They believed that competition for scarce resources was the basic principle of both human and animal adaptation to environment. They wanted to find out if a pattern existed in the formation of an agrarian and feudal society into an urban, industrial and capitalist society. Burgess agued that modern American cities grew in five concentric zones. The inner-most part was the central business district. Just outside this, a second zone developed. This was heavily populated by low income and foreign groups. Zone three was populated by factory workers and clerks. The fourth zone consisted of the residential area of the fairly rich. Outside this zone, away from the city limits, resided the high income groups and this was the fifth zone (Burgess, 1923).

Hoyt proposed sector theory in which he suggested that urban growth took place along the main transportation routes and along lines of least resistance. He visualized city as a circle, various land use areas as sectors radiating from the centre and expanding towards the periphery (U. S. Federal Housing Administration), (Hoyt, 1939). Haris and Ullman modified sector theory of urban growth. According to this theory, various land use patterns in cities developed around several independent nuclei (Haris, C. D. and Ullman, E. C. 1945). Louis Wirth in his famous model of 'urbanization as a way of life' investigated what the impact of the city was on the behavioural patterns or how exactly urban life differed form the rural life. For him, "a city may be defined as a relatively large, dense and permanent settlement of socially heterogeneous individuals" (Wirth, 1980). Large size, density and heterogeneity create certain urban characteristics such as "the substitution of secondary for primary contacts, the weakening of bonds of kinship, the disappearance of the neighbourhood and the undermining of the traditional basis of solidarity" (Wirth, 1980). Urban life leads to a considerable personal disorganization.

Another notable contribution to the ecology of cities is made by Gideon Sjoberg, who made a distinction between pre-industrial and industrial cities (Sjoberg, 1960). The ecological, economic and social organisation of the pre-industrial cities are quite different from those of the industrial cities. The technology of the pre-industrial cities is based on the use of human and animal power, while that of the industrial cities is based on inanimate sources of power. There is a rigid social segregation of people in the pre-industrial city, which is dominated by an elite. Sjoberg thinks that many cities of the developing nations belong to the pre-industrial type.

Central Place Location Theory

Many years ago Sir Flinders Petrie assumed that the only or the main reason for the existence of a city is its function at a storage centre. Geographers still display a tendency to explain the location of urban site in terms of their functions as service centres. An elaborate scheme of this type was offered by a German geographer Walter Christaller. His basic assumption was that a given rural area supports an urban centre which in turn serves the surrounding countryside. Mackenzie was inclined to accept a similar viewpoint when remarking that during this period of population dispersion the city was for the most part, the child and servant of expanding rural settlements. Christaller's view was introduced in America by Mann with modifications.

This theory, however, is patently at variation with facts. Whether we examine the distance between larger cities or the general distribution of urban settlement we find no regularity in spacing. Perhaps the theorists were mainly influenced by the fact of the growth of towns in the beginning as market centres. Mann admits the vulnerability of the scheme for larger places. In highly industrialized areas the central place scheme is generally so distorted by industrial concentration in response to resources and transportation that it may be said to have little significance as an explanation for urban location and distribution.

Sector Theory of Urban Growth

Several attempts have been made to find the principles

which shape the ecological patterns of the city. To find rules which govern equally the spatial development of all urban settlements regardless of time and location seems an ever continuing venture.

The sector theory of Home Hoyt was developed two years after Burgess's theory was tested in relation to the growth of existing cities. According to Hoyt this theory was intended as a modification of Burgess's theory. Hoyt's theory was more dynamic in character than Burgess's proposition since constant changes, populations movements, expansion of industries and their effects on spatial patterns were studied.

As Hoyth's theory is also based on the study of a few cities it suffers from its own drawbacks. It cannot supply us anymore with a universal pattern of the growth of cities. As Hoyt wrongly contends, high class residential areas do not proceed along transportation lines, as high class people prefer to live away from the din of urban traffic. Hoyt's theory does not explain the growth of suburban or satellite townships. It also cannot account for the concept of "twin cities". Moreover, city growth depends upon its location and one cannot expect every other city to be located near high grounds or a water front.

But the sector is definitely a welcome development over the concentric zone theory as it makes room for the modern concept of location of industries also for the growth of a variety of cities wherein the areas of concentric zone are located along side in various sectors. Moreover, it gives importance to city growth around transportation lines which is akin to the modern concept of convenient location of ecological areas of the city.

Urban Sociological Theories

The theoretical offerings of urban sociology constitute a small part of the literature. The classical theories of urban sociology are divided from the works of European Sociologists like Karl Marx, Tonnies, George Simmel, Max Weber and those of American namely, Park Burgess, Louis Wirth and Redfield. Urbanization has became a fact of our every day lives. But the reflection of the earlier sociologists throw light on the anti-urban feelings. The great city, metropolis is a paradigm of an inhuman, debasing, social enviroment for

Tonnies; Simmel felt that the money economy of the cities destroyed social life. Weber and Wirth explained how mass urbanization nullified opportunities or political participation. Charles Booth and Rowntree wrote the "Sociography" of life in the cities. Classical sociologists with the help of economic historians attempted systematic analysis for urbanization as a force for change.

Karl Marx and F. Engles

Marx and Engles condemned the consequences of urbanization under capitalism. They viewed the concentration and immigration of the mass of workers in the new urban agglomerations as a necessary stage in the creation of a revolutionary force. For them pauperization and material degradation was one aspect of urbanization, but equally important was the destruction of the social nexus of the traditional community and its replacement by the utilitarian world of the city. Both for theory and for practice, communism depended on urbanism. Urbanization was liberative. There was nothing to salvage from the urban past, for the social bonds of community were to be replaced first by the new groupings of class and then by the development of human potentiality for its own sake and the true realm of freedom.

There was contemporary pride in the new cities which were seen as engines of progress and the source of all fruitful change. Urbanization was progressive, providing the conditions not only for the transformation of mankind's productive capacities, but also for the realization of individuality. The city offered a market for the special talents of individuals. The spectrum of analysis varied from the Marxian concept of alienation of labour in a productive system based on private property, to the realization of individuality through the sale of labour in a market economy. Freedom for the Marxists could only exist beyond the city, for the liberals this was what the economic development/growth of city life provided. Freedom, diversity and opportunity of choice were the progressive aspects of urbanization.

In the writings of neo-marxists like Mills, Marcuse, Fromm and Fanon there is a consensus that conditions of capitalist urbanization are mutilative of the personality, inhibitive of community formation, destructive of social engagement or involvement and conducive to apathy alienation and anomic. Class consciousness is inhibited and diverted in mass movements, unreason and not reason typifies social response. Urbanization is no longer the sine qua non of a socialist transformation of society. If urbanization is progressively bankrupt in human terms cities themselves are seen as instruments of capitalist or imperialist, domination. The growth of cities depended on the effectiveness of their expropriation of the wealth of their satellites, i. e. their political control. Typically, the characteristic features of the cities is seen not as their economic specialization, but, their role as centres of dominance.

Cities are not only the controlling centres of their societies but also the source of innovation and change. They act as the source of new ideas for production, the leaders of taste, fashion, the pace setters for consumption, guardians of culture and the conservers of order in society. Consensus and continuity in a society are maintained from the city centres. Not only are economic enterprise and political power concentrated there, but so is social authority. To the concepts of expropriation and domination must be added that of hegemony. Hegemony signified authority, the right to rule, intellectual or moral prestige consensus. It has come to mean a social authority whose ultimate sanction is a profound cultural supremacy. The entire society is drawn into the way of life transmitted from the cities so that urbanism, the culture of the city's ruling elites, it diffused throughout. Urban culture becomes the legitimation for control. From Tonnies, Simmel and Wirth there is the same assessment of personality, community and culture in the urban centres. The long standing antagonism between town and country had become a symmetrical relationship in which the countryside was relegated to economic stagnation, poverty and decay of its culture through the loss and pauperization of its population. These thinkers underscore the class basis of urban culture.

Sociologists in a long succession from Tonnies to Wirth were developing a counter-theory of Marxism from the explication of social change led to acceptance of a fundamental cleavage between rural and urban, tradition and modernism which was in sharp opposition to any variant on Marxist theories of development. The urban is accepted as a frame of reference and the urban society as a specific mode of social organization becomes the object of scientific study. Such an orientation of thought did not occur overnight. It took almost half a century from 1887 to 1938 to throw the lingering after effects of the ideological revolution occasioned by Marxism and to explore the full implications of a sociological vocabulary for the study of urbanization.

Ferdinand Tonnies

In the year 1887 Tonnies brought out "Community and Society", the first of the classic sociological texts. He explained the impact of the market economy on traditional forms of social association; the implications of urbanization and the development of the state for the conduct of social life, and the mechanisms of social solidarity in an individualating society. The distinction he draws between the two forms of human association, Gemeinschaft and Gesellschaft, has become the basis for a succession of typologies of which the best known are the pattern variables formulated by Parsons and the folk-urban typology drawn by Redfield and Wirth.

For Tonnies the city of metropolis is the paradigm of bourgeois society. The metropolis represents the culmination of gesellschaft in community life. He present a typology of community life related to two forms of social will; the house, the village and the town representing gemeinschaft community formations derived from blood (the family) place (the neighbourhood) and mind (religion and friendship); whereas the city, the capital city and the metropolis are based on relations of the gesellschaft. In the metropolis, money and capital are unlimited and almighty. It is able to produce and supply goods and science for the entire earth, as well as, laws and public opinion for all nations. It represents the world market and world traffic. World industries are concentrated in it. Its newspapers are world papers, its people from all corners of the earth. To Tonnies the transition from agrarian, parochial Europe to commercial cosmopolitan society had been a bigger break in human experience, than any that a socialist revolution could effect.

The account of urbanization found in this book form the basis of the conventional sociological stereotype later developed by Wirth. The village and the town in which the physical real soil, the permanent location, the visible land, create the strongest ties and relations are compared with the city and metropolis where the continuity and intimacy provided by neighbourhood is broken. The city represents the exaggeration of the principle of space. Localism is replaced by a restless cosmopolitanism, urban, national even international interest replace those of home village and town. In the city only the upper strata the rich and the cultural setup the standards to which the lower strata have to confirm. City life and gesellschaft doom the common people to death and decay. Urbanization leads towards individuation, towards a situation in which each person is his own master; free to move where he will, associate with whom he pleases, for what ever ends he cares to name. Action is undertaken for predicted ends. The "self" of gemeinschaft is replaced by the "person" of gesellschaft. Instead of organic unity of the former we find an aggregate where independent individuals self-conscious maintain in an artificial identity.

The lengthy analysis of the economic relations underlying the new urbanization and the explicit references to class and class domination. Set Tonnies apart from much subsequent sociological discussion of cities and urbanizatio. The influence of Tonnies on the Chicago school of urban sociologist is considerable. Though they accept the direction of social change brought out by urbanization they do not subscribe to Tonnies exchange economy of capitalism and the resultant class structure as the base line of analysis. Urbanization for Tonnies entails the acquiescence of the broad mass of the people in the life styles of the dominant class, while for the Americans (Chicago school) it was considered to bring about assimilation into society. The city's land market, not its exchange economy was considered to be the great leveler.

George Simmel

Simmel's essay "Metropolis and Mental Life" is hailed as "the most important single article on the city from the sociological standpoint" by Wirth. There are five main themes running through the discussion of individual life in metropolitan city. The first of these is that of arousal in face of psychological and socio-psychological stimuli deriving from the turmoil of the urban environment. In consequence a blasé attitude is developed a failure to react to surrounding self. The resultant strategy is that of reserve in face of the superficial and fleeting contact of the crowd. Otherwise one would be complete automised internally and come to an unimaginable nervous state. In fact reserve is essential to social order in the metropolis, and the development of this aversion to others marks the individuals socialization into the city. The large city's heterogeneity and cosmopolitanism requires a certain kind of personality, thoroughly intellectual, remotive, reserved and detached. The urban personality is for Simmel, the basis fo urban culture, or urbanism.

Simmel introduced a subsidiary theme in his essay that of the city as the seat of the highest economic division of labour. Competition induces specialization and hence differentiation and individuality. Urban freedom rested in release from the pettiness and prejudices with in the small town man and the division of labour, specialization was only an incidental feature of the city. The essential feature of urbanization was the freedom it provided for individualization.

Autonomy and individuality of existence in the metropolitan environment constitute the central concern of the essay. Simmel argues that the metropolis offers a kind, and an amount of, freedom which has an analogy whatsoever under conditions, for it has no enlargement of the circle which forms our social milieu. Metropolis is unique in that circle is enlarged by more than the aggregate of the immediate social groups. The city transcends this through its dominance over an ever expanding hinterland and its more important characteristic is thus functional extension beyond its physical boundaries. The number of people in relation extends far beyond the city boundaries and the effective society extends to national and even international horizons. In this characteristic rest the essential cosmopolitanism of the city, the possibility for every individual to work out his own incomparability and particularity.

Simmel's analysis had certain attractions for the urban sociologists because he attempts to define the metropolis and metropolitan culture in sociological terms. His explanation of urbanization is constructed in purely sociological terms. The chain of argument commences with the city as aggregation of individuals. This is in association with money economy, itself considered as series of social transactions, leads to reverse and a blasé attitude nationality and calculability of social life and the division of labour. These in turn are the basis for an urban institutions organisations and culture drive. Urban life is to be explained by the urban personality. To Simmel, urbanization derives the direction from the social relationship set up in the cities and all other social change derives from urbanization.

Max Weber

The lecture papers of Max Weber (1911-1913) were published as "The city". Mumford says that this work of Weber gives the "fullness of understanding of the normal processes of the city further". Robert Park claimed that they were the "closest approximations to a systematic theory of urbanism". Weber's sociological arguments are embedded in a matrix of historical material, which serves as a medium for a sustained critique of the direction taken by urbanization in the western world. Critical of Simmel's economic definition of the city, Weber defines the city on the basis of political and administrative conception.

In his discussion of the emergence of the western city, Max Weber recounts as process in which the development of the rational legal institutions that characterize the modern city enabled the individual to be free from traditional groups, and therefore, develop his individuality. No longer were the means of social control in the city, myth and ritual, nor the immutable and unchallengeable 'cake of custom'. For the first time the oath of citizenship was taken by the individual. Personal membership, not that of kin-group or tribe, in the local, association of the city supplied the legal guarantee of the individual's personal legal position as a burglar.

Weber's study of the city is as central to his investigation of the development of capitalism as his works on religion. Urbanization under specific economic and political circumstances was a necessary linkage in the chain of conditions leaping to capitalism. The medieval city was important in that it had been the basis of the new nations states of Europe as well as modern capitalism. Medieval urban development was the carrier of both of these phenomena and an important factor in their origin.

In Weber's view, the urban settlements of his day had ceased to be cities. There was a state of affairs less civilized than that found in the cities of the late Middle Ages. Much of his description of the medieval city must be seen is an indictment of the direction taken by urbanization in the west. To explain the ideal type of a city Weber selects the perfect case where all men valued the city so highly because it represented their economic and personal freedom that there could be no doubt as to its existence. He attached tremendous importance: on participation in action on behalf of others, through associations. The fate of the western world has been that of the pauperization of public life. The fate of our times (modern time) is characterized by rationalization and intellectualization; and above all by the 'disenchantment of the world': precisely the ultimate and the most sublime values have retreated from public life. His ideal city is, therefore, the relatively closed system of the medieval guild city in which economic enterprise and religious activity, public and private life, are fused. From this standpoint he points to a progressive deterioration in community life with the development of capitalism.

Weber's treatment of the city has limitations in application to contemporary society. It outlines too perfect a conception of urban existence to do more than demonstrate how imperfect on this standard are the present urban settlements. It is an utopian conception and as such lends itself to critique rather than analysis. Its usefulness rests on first its methodology and second, in its delineation of the essential features of social association in the cities of capitalism. He emphasized the city's rationality of organization, the indispensability of formal social controls, such as the law and the police, the secularization the predominance of impersonal contractual relationships and its individualism. The city is a free association in which the individual participates in his personal right. And finally the city is dominated by bourgeoisie. The secular rational, individualist, market oriented community formations of the medieval cities derived from and permitted the activities and interest of this new class.

Robert Redfield

Redfield's book "The Folk Culture of Yucatan" gives complete report of the field work and the theoretical exposition of the folk-urban continuum. Field work in the Yucatan peninsula of Mexico was carried out by Redfield from 1927 to 1936. Four communities (Merida, Dzitas, Chan kom and Tusik) were studied representing distinct points of development from a folk to an urban society. Redfield wrote that "the chief objective of the investigation is to define differences in the nature of isolated homogeneous society on the one hand, and mobile heterogeneous society on the other so far as these kinds of societies are represented in Yucatan". Redfield argued that these four communities represented a real and continuous process of social change indicating stages of urban development. Close comparison of their differences suggested to Redfield, the presence in varying degrees of particular variables which supported his theory of folk-urban continuum. He had identified the strategic variables that separated folk from urban society.

According to Redfield there are three major categories of urban change: (a) the increase in cultural disorganizations; (b) the increase in secularization and (c) the increase in individualization. He saw cultural disorganization as a concomitant of urbanization because he believed that the strong ties that integrated the individual into the folk or peasant community were inevitably loosened or destroyed by the growth of urban society. "Folk society in which the same kind of people are doing the same kind of thing" created an unambiguous, monolithic social structure which was destroyed by the growth of the city. The single social fabric of meanings typical of folk communities which torn and replaced by that of the numerous goals, actions and meanings of urban society. The wholeness of folk culture in which all cultural elements were related, became a cultural patch work in urban society. As a result conflict and disorganization were the marks of urban culture.

Cities and towns were secular in their values than were villages. Secularization lessened the importance of the Church and of the religion in society and emphasized rational and practical judgments. The individual was free from traditional control. Collective functions disappeared and individual activity increased in the urban society. The extended family with its wide spread network of obligations, was reduced to a small, secular and self-contained unit. Decline of religion and its control gave the individual more freedom from social ties of the folk society. Urbanization increased individualization. Redfield's folk-urban continuum explains the process of evolutionary changes, which describes how little communities give way to larger, urban secular society.

Louis Wirth

In 1938 Louis Wirth wrote one of the classics in the literature on "Urbanism as a way of life". He had a sense of prophecy that came from a deep understanding of the subjects that concerned him including race relation, ecology, urban planning and urban theory. At that time there was not even a clearly defined sociological orientation to the study of urban society. With regard to a lack of theoretical orientation he wrote; "In the rich literature on the city we look in vain for a theory systematizing the available knowledge concerning the city as a social entity; we do indeed have excellent formulations of theories on special problems ... and we have a wealth of literature presenting insights of sociological relevance and empirical studies offering detailed information on a variety of particular aspects of urban life. But despite the multiplication of research and text book on the city we do not yet have a comprehensive body of competent hypothesis which may be derived from a set of postulates implicitly contained in a sociological definition of the city".

The core of Wirth's essay on urbanism contained three assumptions from which other propositions were deduced, size, density and heterogeneity were the causes of urban characteristics. Wirth argued that large numbers permitted a wide range of individual variations and an increase in the potential differentiation within the population. The larger the group or community, the greater the variations it contained. The greater the variation the greater the increase in spatial segregation by colour, ethnic, heritage and status. Spatial segregation weakened the bonds of kinship, neighbourliness and the sentiments arising out of living together for generations under a force the substitution of competition and formal controls for the earlier informal bonds that held folk society together.

Wirth initiated another series of proposition using the concept of size. The increase in numbers limits the possibility of each member of the community knowing all the other personality. The limitation of personal interaction encourages the development of segmentalized social contacts by which urbanites come to know fewer people and to know them less intimately than would be the case in a small community. Urbanities do not become involved with one another as total personalities but in specialised segments, interaction being primarily for definite and instrumental reasons. This feature of the urban society increases the superficiality, anonymity and the transitory character of urban social relationships. In urban society the individual gains a certain degree of emancipation or freedom from the personal and emotional controls of intimate groups. He loses the spontaneous self-expression, the morale and the sense of participation that comes with living in an integrated society. The segmented life of urban society is more likely to exposed the urban residents to feelings of anomie, to a sense of personal disorganization and to a loss of spontaneity. Size has been the single level to raise a number of conclusions about urban society.

Wirth has also analysed density also as a basic characteristic or urban society. Density increased the social and psychological effects created by size. It intensified the need for specialization and differentiation. It underlined the need for formal control to counteract irresponsibility and potential disorder that were assumed to develop from that fact of large numbers in urban society. Density increased the tendency towards spatial segregation that is, towards social group in the city separating themselves and forming relatively homogeneous neighbourhoods.

Heterogeneity is a consequence of size and density. It developed principally as a social response to economic necessity. Interaction of individuals from different backgrounds destroyed the rigid divisions of the smaller integrated society and introduced a more complex pattern of social stratification. Heterogeneity led to greater mobility, geographic as well as social. It also produced a counter tendency by which a certain amount of social leveling occurred inspite of the wide variation found in the city. The leveling was accomplished by means of standardization of consumer goods and the standardization of beliefs. These forms of standardization, in turn increased the impersonality of social intercourse in the city because urban residents came more or less to have common opinions and to react to one another in terms of stereotyped conceptions. When large number of persons have to make common use of facilities and institutions, those facilities and institutions must serve the needs of the average persons rather than those of particular individuals. If the individual would participate at all in the social, political and economic life of the city, he must subordinate some of his individuality to the demands of the larger community and in that measure lose himself in mass movements. All these three sociological perspectives of urbanization viz. Park & Burge's 'Ethnicity', Redfield's 'Folk-Urban Continuum' and Louis Wirth's 'Urbanism as a way of life' have been used as conceptual tools in the dissertation.

URBAN CLASSIFICATION AND DEMOGRAPHIC TRENDS IN INDIA

The term 'urban' has been defined in various ways by many scholars. It can be defined in terms of political status, demographic attributes (size and/or density), economic variables (the prevalence of non-agricultural occupations), socio-cultural pattern of behaviour independent of sustenance activities and even psychological characteristics.

Urban centres defined in demographic terms, for example, may indeed manifest considerable political, economic, socio-cultural and psychological diversities. However, this would be true for any definition of an urban centre in terms of one attribute. This is not to suggest that only one attribute should be used to define cities for a particular type of analysis.

The concept of 'urban' and 'rural' areas originate from the way of life and activities of their inhabitants. Normally, an urban centre differs from the rural in terms of the occupation of its population, which is not concerned directly with farming. Some scholars suggest that the rural are those sections of the people who are spread over the countryside, and are engaged in the production of the primary necessities from the soil, whereas the urban sections are those dense clusters of persons who have no immediate interest in the production of materials for their food and clothing or general comfort, but are engaged in transport, manufacturing, buying and selling goods or in educating the people or in managing the affairs of the state or in merely 'living in town'.

R. Murphy defines the urban area as busy streets lined with houses, stores, factories and the like, whereas the term rural connotes the open countryside with farm houses and their surrounding fields or even expanses of woods and wastelands (Murphy, 1972). But actually, urban areas often grade almost imperceptibly into rural areas; there is no natural or universally recognized boundary between them. Consequently in recent years, the line that is drawn between urban and rural for statistical or census purposes is necessarily arbitrary. There is no clear cut distinction between a city and the country.

The definition of urban population, most widely used, is based on the size of the place. An urban place is distinguished from a rural agglomeration by having a larger population and a considerable degree of division of labour in both industrial production and services. Hence, the criterion of the size of population of a place and the percentage of non-agricultural population should be applied to define urban population. In order to define urban population, the lower limit of urban population may range from 300 to 20,000, above which a place is considered to be urban.

In different countries, different sizes of population have been taken into consideration for outlining urban status. In the United States, an urban place must have a population of at least 2500 and in Canada 1000. But in Canada, some places with as few as 200 people rank as urban, whereas in Japan the population size of an urban centre consists of more than 20,000. In France, a place is regarded as urban only if it contains a clustered of population of at least 2000 at the centre. In Denmark, a settlement consisting of 200 people constitutes a town; in Greece and Venezuela, a place must have over 10,000 inhabitants before it can be called a town; while in Ghana the figure drops to 5000 only. Holland with 20,000 inhabitant and Iceland with only 300 inhabitant mark out the wide variation in the consideration of a town.

In more advanced countries, the greater percentage of people of the town are engaged in services instead of producing material goods (primary occupation). In Britain, half of the working population is engaged in the primary activities and the other half earn their living from buying and selling goods, transferring them from one place to another, or discharging various kinds of personal services, as in professions, entertainment, the transport of an increasingly mobile population, or administering the greatly expanded social services. But now in Great Britain and U.S.A., the non-producers (other than primary) are in a majority. In the countries such as Poland and Yugoslavia, more than three-fourths of the population are still engaged in primary activities, most of them in agriculture. A country like China shows an even greater preponderance of producers. In Russian towns, one-fourth workers were engaged in service occupation by 1963. In Japan, the service sector has reached 40 percent . Australia has nearly as high a proportion in services as Great Britain, and in the U. S. A. the process has gone even further.

Attributes of the Cities in India

In 1881 census, every place with a population of 5000 persons or more was treated as a town, whether it had any urban characteristics or not. In 1891 census, the Census authorities went to the other extreme in deciding which place should be treated as urban, and no place was so treated unless it was under a municipal administration. The census definition of town appears to be more or less the same during the period 1901-51, and it was only in 1961 that several modifications were introduced to make the definition more flexible from the statistical point of view. However, although the definition of 'town' has remained the same all through the decades 1901-51, uniformity has not always been maintained in the application of this definition.

The definition of a town given in the Imperial census of India, 1901 is as follows: Towns include (i) every municipality of whatever size, (ii) all civil lines not included within municipal limits and (iii) every other continuous collection of houses, permanently inhabited by not less than 5000 persons which the provincial Superintendent may decide to treat as a town for census purposes. Thus, the primary consideration for deciding a town was its administration set-up and not the size of its population. The Commissioner of the 1911 census points out that "in framing the definition, the object in view was as far as possible to treat as towns only places which are of a more or less urban character". But there was no specified list of urban characteristics, no specified directions were given to Census Superintendents about the applicability of these tests and everything was left to the discretion of the census authorities. The commissioner of 1921 census enumerates "the provincial superintendent will have regard to the character of the population, the relative density of the dwelling, the importance of the place as a centre of trade and its historic associations, and will bear in mind that it is undesirable to treat as towns overgrown villages which have no urban characteristics". The definition of town adopted in the 1951 census, reads – a town is normally an inhabited locality with a total population of not less than 5000 persons. But places with a somewhat larger population which do not possess definite urban character may not be treated as towns. At the same time, places with a smaller population with definite urban character (including generally all municipalities and cantonments and other places having a local administration of their own) may be treated as separate towns. The decision in marginal cases rests with State Governments in some states and census superintendents in others.

Identifying Cities in Independent India

In adopting a definite criteria the 1961 census seems to be much more rigorous than in earlier censuses and further, this definition has been followed all over India as uniformly as the circumstances could permit. The census towns have been determined on the basis of a number of emperical tests: (i) a density of not less than 1000 per sq. mile; (ii) a population of 5000; (iii) three-fourths of the occupation should be outside of agriculture; (iv) the place should have, according to the census superintendent of the state, a few pronounced urban characteristics and amenities, the definition of which, although leaving room for vagueness and discretion, yet meant to cover newly founded industrial areas, large housing settlements, or places of tourist importance which were recently served with all civic amenities.

The definition of 1961 census has been retained in 1971 also. But according to the 1981 census, an urban unit denotes as follows.– (a) All places with municipal corporation, municipality, notified area committee, cantonment boards, etc.; (b) All places which satisfy the following criteria – (i) A minimum population of 5000; (ii) At least 75 percent of the male working population being engaged in non-agricultural pursuits and (iii) A density of population of at least 400 persons per sq. km.

The definition of an urban unit at the 2001 census in India is as follows:

a. All places with a municipality, corporation, cantonment board or notified town area committee, etc.

b. All other places which satisfied the following criteria:

   i. A minimum population of 5000;

   ii. At least 75 percent of the male working population engaged in non-agricultural pursuits; and

   iii. A density of population of at least 400 per sq.km. (1,000 per sq. mile).

The same definition was adopted at the 1991 census also. This will ensure comparability with previous censuses and provide the basis for analysis of urbanization trends in the country. On the basis of the above criteria two distinct types of urban area emerged. The first type is a group of towns notified by the state Government under special Acts and is known as Statutory Towns. The second type is based on the fulfillment of the demographic criteria stated in (b) above and is known as Census Towns. While applying the test of occupation of the male working population male main workers engaged in the agricultural activities, namely, Cultivators, Agricultural Labourers and Livestock, Forestry, Fishing and Plantations, Orchards, etc. are excluded for computing the percentage of workers engaged in non-agricultural occupation.

The following are the possible different situation in which urban agglomerations would be constituted.

i. A city or town with one or more contiguous outgrowths;

ii. Two or more adjoining towns with their outgrowths; and

iii. A city and one or more adjoining towns with their outgrowths all of which form a continuous spread.

The concept of 'Urban Agglomeration' has been introduced in census studies for the first time in 1971 in India. The definition, adopted in 1971, has been still retained. An 'urban agglomeration' has been defined as "a continuous urban spread constituted of a town and its adjoining urban outgrowth or two or more physically contiguous towns together with continuous well organised urban outgrowths, if any, of such towns". Since there is considerable socio-economic interrelationship between such physically contiguous urban units, it has been considered purposeful to group them under an urban agglomeration.

The classification of town and cities has many dimensions. Social demographers, sociologists, geographers, economists, historians, town planners etc., have made their own classification of towns considering different aspects. The sociologists and economists take mainly the demographic, occupational, industrial, cultural and social factors. Sociologists like Marcel Aurousseau, Redfield and Singer, Pierenne, Sjoberg have tried to classify the towns on their functional basis. Redfield and Singer classify them into two parts (i) Orthogenitic, (ii) Heterogenitic on the basis of socio-cultural variables (Redfield, and Singer, 1954). Pierenne divides them into political intellectual and other economic centres. Gideon Sjoberg classify them into pre-industrial and industrial towns, the former have been in existence for the last so many centuries and have a rural and traditional background and the latter, which have recently developed after the advent of industry (Sjoberg, 1960). Taking into account the nature and function of cities sociologists especially Hozelitz has divided them into generative and parasitic (Hozelitz, 1955).

Taking size as the basic criterion for classification, the census of India has classified towns and cities into six classes. Class I towns contains one lakhs persons and above, class II has a population between, 50,000 to 99,999, class III towns contains 20,000 to 49,999, class IV towns have population between 10,000 to 19,999, class V towns contains 5,000 to 9,999 and class VI towns have less than 5,000 population.

If a place does not satisfy all the three pre-requisites for a census town then in such cases the determining factor has been either the administrative significance of the place or its historical or cultural importance or the fact that the place has tourist importance. Areas which have been neither notified by the state government nor identified by the Directorate of census operations as urban are rural. Cities and towns are determined in terms of the size of inhabitant and structure of their population. In India, a city may be regarded as a relatively large sized urban community with complex socio-economic and cultural diversities. A town which has more than one lakh inhabitant is called a city (class I town) and more than ten lakhs, a metropolitan city.

Trends of Urbanization in India

So far as the urbanization from demographic point of view is concerned, i.e. the proportion of population living in towns and cities, India is in the midst of gigantic urban increase. In India, 80 percent population is rural and 20 percent urban (1981). From 1901 to 2001 there has been a slow but steady growth of urbanization which is shown in Table 1.1.

Table 1.1
Trends of Urbanisation in India: 1901-2001

Census Year	No. of Towns	Total population (In millions)	Urban population (In millions)	Urban population as % of total population	Decadal growth of urban populaton %
1901	1827	238.40	25.85	10.84	-
1911	1815	252.09	25.94	10.29	0.35
1921	1949	251.32	28.09	11.18	8.27
1931	2072	278.98	33.46	11.99	19.12
1941	2250	318.66	44.15	13.86	31.97
1951	2843	361.09	62.44	17.29	41.42
1961	2365	439.23	78.94	17.97	26.41
1971	2590	548.16	109.11	19.91	38.23
1981	3378	683.33	159.46	23.34	46.14
1991	3768	844.32	217.18	25.74	36.19
2001	5161	1,027.01	285.35	27.79	31.13

Sources: Census of India.

Urban centres in India, however, have grown in a faster rate, because of the low living standards of a large population who migrate to the urban places in search of livelihood. The growth of urban centres was relatively slow from 1901 until 1941, increasing from 10.84 percent to 13.86 percent of the total population thus raising the growth of urban population to 37.97 percent from 25.85 million to 44.15 millions, with the number of towns increasing from 1827 to 2250.

In 1951, the urban population grew to about 41.42 percent which comprises 44.15 million or 17.97 percent of the total population, with then umber of towns also increasing rapidly to 2843. In between 1951 to 1961, the urban population increased only by less than 1 percent i.e 17.29 percent to 17.97 percent of the total population showing a decline in the urban population (41.42 percent to 26.41 percent) and the number of towns (2843 to 2365). During 1961-71 decade, the urban population increased from 78.94 million to 109.11 million with a growth of 38.23 percent in the urban population. During 1971-81, the urban population increased rapidly to 46.14 percent consisting of 159.46 million persons of urban population with 3379 number of towns. In 1981-2001 decade, though the number of towns increased from 3378 to 5161 and the urban population increased from 159.46 million to 285.35 million, consisting about 23.34 percent to 27.97 percent of the total population. However, within this decade there has been a decline in the growth of urban population from 36.19 percent to 31.13 percent as indicated in Table 1.1.

Distribution of Urban Population and Towns in Norht East India

North East India, one of the strategic regions of our country consists of seven states. The region covers an area of 255,000 sq. m, which constitutes approximately 7.7 percent of the geographical area of the country and about 4 percent of the population (1991). The region has lower level of urbanisation. Taking the percentage of urban population, the North East region of India lags far behind the rest of India. The share of the urban population in the North East is 15.20 percent as against the all India average of 27.79 percent according to 2001 census. Though the percentage of urban population is low, urban growth has been quite impressive in the region during 1981-2001 decade. When we compare the urban situation of all the North Eastern States form 1981-2001 census, all the States except Manipur and Nagaland have made gain both in the percentage of urban population and number of towns (Table 1.2).

Table 1.2
Distribution of Urban Populatoin and Towns in North East: 1981-2001

States	1981 Census		1991 Census		2001 Census	
	Population %	No. of Towns	Population %	No. of Towns	Population %	No. of Towns
Arunachal Pradesh	6.56	6	12.21	10	20.41	17
Assam	10.29	66	11.08	87	12.72	125
Manipur	26.42	32	27.69	30	23.88	33
Meghalaya	18.07	7	18.69	7	19.63	16
Mizoram	24.67	6	46.20	22	49.50	22
Nagaland	15.25	7	17.88	9	17.74	9
Tripura	10.99	10	15.27	18	17.02	23
N. E. India	11.92	134	13.97	183	15.20	245

Sources: Census of India.

The distribution of urban population and towns in Mizoram shows a spectacular increase. The percentage of urban population has almost doubled. In 1981 it was 24.67 percent and in 1991 it reached 46.20 percent. But in 1991-2001 decade shows only a slight increase in the percentage ie. 46.20 in 1991 to 49.50 in 2001. Comparing the number of towns in Mizoram, there were only 6 towns in 1981 and it grew to 22 towns in 1991. However, the growth of towns remains stagnant in the 1991-2001 decade showing no increase whatsoever as the figure remained the same. Arunachal Pradesh also shows a spectacular growth which rose from 6.56 percent in 1981 to 20.41 percent in 2001. The number of towns also increased from 6 in 1981 to 10 in 2001. The State of Tripura also shows a slight increase in the percentage of urban population and towns. In 1981, it was 10.99 percent and in 2001 it reached 17.02 percent. There were only 10 towns in 1981 and in 2001 it reached 18 towns. Assam and Meghalaya can be regarded as the least urbanized states in North East India. In Assam, the urban population shows a slight increase from 10.29 percent in 1981 to 12.72 percent in 2001. But the number of towns shows a spectacular increase from 66 numbers in 1981 to 125 in 2001. Meghalaya has almost remained stagnant in the percentage of urban population and also in the number of towns. Both in 1981 and 1991 the urban population remained almost the same i. e. 18.07 percentand 18.69 percent respectively. In 2001, however, the percentage of urban population in Meghalaya shows a slight increase touching 19.63 percent along with the increase in the number of towns from 7 to 16.

The urban scenario in Manipur shows a slight increase in the urban population from 26.42 percent in 1981 to 27.69 percent in 1991. But the growth of urban population decreased to 23.88 percent in 2001. The number of towns also remained unchanged. In 1981-91 it shows a slight decrease from 32 to 30 numbers respectively and a slight increase to 33 numbers in 2001. Same is the case with Nagaland, with little increase in the urban population from 15.25 percent in 1981 to 17.88 percent in 1991. But if we compare the 1991 and 2001 census, it shows that the urban population has decreased from 17.88 percent to 17.74 percent with the number of towns remaining almost the same with 7 numbers in 1981, 9 numbers in 1991 and there was no increase in the number of towns in 1991-2001 decade.

Therefore, we can say that the distribution of urban population and towns in the different states of North East India has been very much uneven, but as a whole, there has been remarkable increase both in terms of percentage and urban population along with the number of towns.

From Table 1.3 it is evident that between the last 30 years the urban population in the state of Meghalaya has increased from 14.55 percent to 19.67 percent. It may be

Table 1. 3
Three Decades of Urban Growth in Meghalaya and Shillong

	MEGHALAYA		SHILLONG	
Years	Urban Population	Percentage of Urban population	Urban Population	Percent of Shillong in urban Population of the state
1971	1,47,170	14.55	1,22,752	12.13
1981	2,41,333	18.07	1,74,703	13.07
1991	3,30,047	18.60	2,23,366	12.58
2001	4,53,612	19.67	2,67,881	11.61

Source: Census of India.

seen that share of urban percent of population from Shillong in 1971 to 2001 was ranged between 12.13 percent (1971) to 11.61 percent (2001). That suggests a marginal decrease. But 1981 census reported 13.07 percent of urban population in the city of Shillong, which is the recorded figure during the past 30 years. Therefore, it can be said that the percentage of urban population is increasing. However, share of city of Shillong in the urban population of the state is decreasing with slow rise of urban centres in Meghalaya. Still every eight urban residents of Meghalaya lives in Shillong.

URBANIZATION IN INDIA AND NORTH EAST INDIA

The history of India's urbanization dates back to the Indus valley civilization. There existed several cities in India even before the arrival of the British. The Pre-British cities could be classified into four types, namely the religious, capital, educational and commercial or trade cities. Banaras, Prayag (Allahabad) etc., were great religious centres. Patliputra

(Patna), Ayodhya, Dwarka, Agra, Delhi, Fatehpur, Kannauj, Lahore, Dacca, Bidar, Vijayanagara, Kanchipuram, Madurai, Tiruvanantapuram and Mysore were great capital cities. Nalanda, Taxila and Vikramasila were great university centres. Calicut and Cambay were flourishing port cities. Many capital and port cities were also trade centres. Capital cities like Patliputra and Vijayanagara had a population of more than a million during those days (Ghurye, 1962). The rise and fall of capital cities were dependent on the rise and fall of dynasties.

Two of the consequences of the British influence were the growth of population in cities catering to import and export trade and the production of consumer goods. This second stage, however, came much later. Another aspect of this influence was the change in the architectural design of buildings and the introduction of modern utilities. By far the greatest change came in the alteration of the economic and political organization of the urban society. The construction of transportation and communication networks also affected the pattern of urbanization in India. Indian urbanism has essentially been shaped by three civilizations: the Hindu during the early period, the Muslim during the Medieval period and the Christian during the modern period. The rulers representing these civilizations tried to impose elements of their culture on the urban life of India.

India's urbanism has attracted the attention of many scholars including Max Weber, Arnold Toynbee, Patric Geddes, Milton Singer, Robert Redfield, G. S. Ghurye, Gideon Sjoberg and Percival Spear. Max Weber (1962) offered a comparative historical account of the cities, with special attention to the institution of caste in the context of Indian cities. According to him, the caste system obstructed the emergence of citizenry, social and legal equality, fraternization and autonomy of Indian cities. It is the same institution which may account for the continuity of the main structural characteristics of the traditional cities and, to a certain degree, the contemporary cities of India. (Gandhi, Raj. 1983).

Sjoberg (1964) worked out a typology of preindustrial and industrial cities considering industrialization as a key variable based on his data on medieval European and Asian cities. M.S.A. Rao (1974) does not agree with Sjoberg and argues that in the Indian context, the process and growth of urbanization have been so complex that it would be simplistic to characterize the difference in terms of any one factor. He thinks that a general distinction between traditional and modern urbanization may, however, be made in the Indian historical context.

Patric Geddes (1949) conceived of cities as concrete images of civilization. Ghurye illustrated this proposition with reference to ancient Indian cities. Toynbee evinced considerable interest in the study of the location and shifting of capital cities in ancient India, while Ghurye primarily concentrated on the ecological, political and cultural aspects of ancient and medieval cities in the context of civilization, Redfield and Singer worked out, in concrete terms, the social organization of the Great Tradition, sacred geography and they elaborated the function of cities in terms of their cultural role.

In India urbanization has come to occupy an important place in economic development of the country. It is quite often said that 'India lives in her huts and cottages of olden days' but it is also true that India has a tradition of urban living and town planning which goes back to 5000 years. The cities of Indus valley civilization, Mohenjodaro and Harrapa, which flourished 5000 years back, were large and well planned cities. The Indus valley people had attained high standards of town planning and architectural style. Hence in India the urban tradition continued through the century and during the ancient period of our history there were many large well planned and beautiful cities in different parts of the country. Patliputra of Chandragupta Maurya, Ujjain of the Guptas, Kannauj, Banaras and Mathura were some of the great cities in northern India. In the south, great cities were built in the medieval period by the Chalukyas, the Rashtrakutas, the Cholas, the Hoysalas and others. Indeed, the southern tradition can be seen to continue through vijayanagar which flourished during the 15th and 16th centuries to modern Mysore and Bangalore.

The Muslims and later the British made their own distinctive contributions to the evolution of cities in India.

Many of our cities especially those in the north Indian plains bear the imprint of the Muslim influence. The metropolitan port cities like Calcutta, Bombay and Madras are the outstanding examples of British contribution. The cities like Delhi and Bangalore represent a synthesis of different traditions both indigenous and foreign including Hindu, Muslim and British. Thus, the cities that arose in Pre-British India were few in number and archaic in type. They did not rest primarily upon industrial and commercial development but rather on political and religious functions. The Muslim rulers frequently shifted the seat of government, and when they did so the capital city suddenly dwindled to nothing and a new city arose around the next administrative head-quarter. Cities also arose at strategic points where military required a permanent camp, such as bridge heads, mountain passes and cross-roads. Still other cities arose at religious sites where pilgrimages were made and temples were built. In this way for a longtime commerce and industry followed the cities located for non-economic reasons. Modern city has come to prominence just recently, based on industry, trade and natural resources. This new type indicates that urbanization is going on in India in fast rate in comparison with the ancient period.

Hence both in the past and the present religious and administrative centres as a matter of fact acted as an important urbanizing force. Sacred towns emerged on the banks of a holy river, close to a temple or in association with religious personalities as for example Amritsar, Ajmer, Haridwar, Puri and Deoghar. Some of these sacred places in course of time proved to be important cultural centres and principal seats of learning. In modern period industrial and commercial factors become the prime consideration towards urban development. Trade, commerce and industries are influencing a number of towns of small, medium and large size. Regional development is more dependent on the easy means of communication lines, as for example Mirzapur, Modinagar, Kanpur and Jamshedpur. The safety from the menace of rivers and the development of irrigation and power schemes of various 'plans', further led to the growth of varied types of urban centres in the region. A number of new mill towns in the western drier states of U.P., Haryana and the Punjab on the one hand and on the other a number of frontier guard towns or check posts with industrial-cum-commercial activities have grown up recently along the border zone of north India. Towns also grew along the railway lines, which are especially noted for their busy railway activities. In southern India most of the cities have been developed as port, e.g., Bombay, Ernakulam, Madras, Vishakapatnam, Tutikorin, Marmogoa, etc.

As far as the nature and trend of urban studies in India is concerned, the picture is quite different. There are abundant data on socio-economic conditions of individual Indian cities. Rapid urbanization in India since 1941 with its attendant problems stimulated a number of surveys and research efforts. The study of Poona (1945 and 1952) and similar other comprehensive studies conducted by the Gokhale Institute set the pattern for many of the subsequent studies. The Planning Commission of India, through its Research Programmes Committee, sponsored a number of studies on the social and economic conditions in about twenty-two cities in India. These surveys of individual cities, many of them published, constitute the largest collection of material on individual cities in any developing area. The major impetus to urban studies in India came from UNESCO. In 1952 it sponsored a comparative study of in-migration to cities in several south Asian countries. These studies were published as the social implications of industrialization and urbanization (1956).

The 1951 census presented, for the first time, detailed data for the urban and rural population separately and the 1961 census data on the place of birth of migrants and length of stay in the city of enumeration. Publication of this material led to a series of demographic exercises and inventory studies in India (Ghurye:1953; Nath: 1955; Guha: 1958; Sovani: 1954; Ashish Bose: 1959 and Zachariah: 1964). In addition to these demographic studies, several regional and urban geographical studies were also undertaken (Ahmed: 1956; R.K. Singh: 1955 and 1956; D. Mukherjee: 1956; Alam: 1956 and Tiwari: 1958) and produced significant material on spatial relations, economic activity, public institutions and the relationship of the city proper with its hinterland. Hoselitz considers these studies in urban geography superior to the studies in 'urban sociology' and 'social ecology' because of the formers methodological clarity.

Some of the modern and industrial cities of India like Baroda (Malkani: 1957), Calcutta (Bose: 1958, Sen: 1960), Surat (R.P.C.: 1957-59), Poona (Sovani: 1956), Jamshedpur (Mishra: 1959), Hyderabad (Iyengar: 1957), Bombay (Lakhadawala: 1962), Lucknow (Mukherjee and Singh: 1961), Kanpur (Mazumdar: 1960), Ranchi (Vidyarthi: 1960) etc., were studied by some of the social scientists, with the support from R. P. C. of the Planning Commission, Government of India.

Thus, in India different phases of history have given birth to several kinds of towns and cities and the process of urbanization has been in operation since time immemorial. However, the study of urbanization is of very recent concern for the social scientists in India, but several noteworthy publications on India's urbanism have appeared during the past few decades. An important work on urbanism in early historical India is A. Ghosh's The City in Early Historical India (1973). Some of the contributors on urbanism in the medieval period include Edward C. Dimock and Robert B. Inden (1970) who dealt with urbanism in medieval Bengal as revealed in the Mangala Kavya Literature. Gavin Hambly (1968) and Hameeda Khatoon Nagvi (1971) have written on urbanism and urbanization during the Mughal period. The two important publications dealing with urbanism in colonial India are those by A.D. King (1976) and Satish Saberwal (1978). Anthony King studied the evolution of Delhi under British rule and Satish Saberwal's paper on the socio-historical prespective of Indian urbanism focuses largely on issues bearing upon stratification.

Though a vast array of papers and books have been produced in different aspects of urbanization in India, the number of studies relating to the north-east region of India is not numerous. Studies on urbanization in the north-eastern region is not many. However, a beginning was made. S.M. Dube (1971) carried out a project on the process of urbanization in the tribal areas of the North-East. Goswamy's

'Cultural profile of Shillong' (1978) contains interesting papers on various communities, land system and city administration. Another book on Shillong focusing on geographical and spatial analysis, is contributed by J. P. Singh (1980). A. C. Mohapatra (1980) has produced a report on the growth of urban population in the North East from 1951 to 1981 and has compiled data from census reports on district wise and state wise urban population. Hill cities of Eastern Himalayas by A. C. Sinha et.al (1993) examines the land relation, inter-ethnic issues and civic participation at the urban level among the hill states of the region. This study finds that most of the towns located in the hill states of the region such as Cherrapunje, Shillong, Jowai, Tura, Dimapur, Kohima, Mokukchung, Aizawl and Itanagar were studied through an inter-disciplinary approach in which Anthropologists, Historians, Geographers and Sociologists examined the urban phenomena on a common format. Urbanization and Development in North East India by J. B. Ganguly (1995) was an outcome of a seminar, where various scholars had contributed on urban growth of this region.

STRATEGY AND METHOD OF THE STUDY

Statement of the Problem

It is commonly believed that urban people have modern outlook compared to the rural people who are bound by their past tradition. Urban centres are occupied by a number of communities co-existing with each other. Normally the urban people are more educated than their rural counterparts. Thus, it will be interesting to understand the problem of multi-ethnic co-existence of an educated and modern society in an urban setting such as Shillong. The proposed study of urban social structure will encompass, the above concerns.

Objectives of the study

It is claimed that urbanization brings modernity and cosmopolitan outlook among its citizens. The city of Shillong as the premiere and most cosmopolitan city of North-east is known for its multi ethnic settlements. Therefore it is sociologically significant to understand the character of the social set up in this background. Thus, it is proposed to study the following aspects of city of Shillong:

1. To understand the urban social structure of Shillong.
2. To examine the pattern of interaction among the ethnic groups.
3. To comment on the nature of modernity prevalent in Shillong.
4. To uncover the efforts of the State on urban development.

Construction and Finalisation of the Questionnaire

The questionnaire was constructed carefully in the light of other questionnaires which were available. The questionnaire thus constructed were both closed and open ended or in an un-restricted form. The closed type was selected because of the fact that they were easy to respond, they take little time, they keep the respondent on the subject and they are fairly easy to tabulate and analyse.

The questionnaire was first tried out on 20 respondents of both the localities of the study area in the month of September 2001. In order to determine the suitability of the instrument. The findings of the try-out actually indicate the efficiency of tools and also suggest the necessary modification to be incorporated in the items as well as the instrument before conducting the final study. After getting back the try out questionnaires, the investigator thus felt the necessity of improving and validating the questionnaire. Accordingly the questionnaire was revised and some needed modifications were incorporated.

After analysing the items on the basis of expert criticism and in the light of try out results, the next step was to administer the questionnaire to a large representative sample of the population to collect the desired data for carrying out the present study. The selected items were arranged systematically.

The final administration of the questionnaire was done in the month of October to December 2001. The investigator introduced himself to every respondent and the purpose of study was explained. The investigator requested the kind cooperation from the respondents. They were also given the necessary direction for filling up the questionnaire.

Sampling Design Field Strategy

We have made use of the sampling technique for collection of primary data. Two localities have been purposely chosen as the sample of the study with a view to provide adequate representation of the city of Shillong in view of their locations and the inhabitants occupying these areas. The sample for the present study includes two urban localities of Shillong: (a.) Laitumkhrah (an ethnically heterogeneous unit) and (b.) Jaiaw (an ethnically compact/homogenous unit).

The Laitumkhrah locality has a mixed population of various ethnic, linguistic, religious and regional communities. Jaiaw on the other hand is pre-dominantly a Khasi tribal locality. Both these localities fall under the control of the Shillong Municipal Board and have a long urban history. So, taking these factors into consideration the two areas have been accordingly selected for extensive study.

With a view to identifying the respondents for interviewing, every fourth household was chosen as a unit from one end of the locality. Care was taken to exclude all non-residential structures from being selected as a sample unit for obvious reason. The respondents were the adult heads of the household in both the localities. In their absence, because of unavoidable reasons, the next adult was taken as a substitute for administering the questionnaire.

The chosen technique for identifying the individual respondents, led to 131 households from Jaiaw and another 147 households in Laitumkhrah. The heads of these households were served with the questionnaires and their responses on them were collected in course of time after repeated visits to their residence. After collecting back the questionnaire, we found that some answers in the questionnaire were vague, contradictory and incomplete. In fact, in some of the questionnaires the respondents had just filled in sometimes their names and addresses and sometime upto the other social background data, but critical questions remained unanswered. With a view to removing distortions from our analyses, we decided to exclude such incompletely answered questionnaires. And that's how we managed to get a list of 215 completed questionnaires for statistical analysis. We presume that an analysis of these collected data from the two localities will be applicable to the urban phenomena of the city of Shillong at large. And we shall be able to make general statements on the pattern of human behaviour, urban social structure and the nature of modernity of Shillong.

For secondary sources, the collection of information was based on the review of relevant literature, journals and magazines, newspapers, research works, surveys conducted by various organizations, District Statistical Handbook, books, official and unofficial records, Census Reports etc. Thus, both primary and secondary sources of data were used to understand the complexity of urban Shillong.

We would like to add a few words about the field work. Due to non-availability of some of the respondents, who were busy persons in their lives and were not in station, we had to wait for them for longer period of time. Some of the respondents, who had not as yet experienced this kind of study, took time in giving information needed by the investigator on the questionnaires. Regarding collection of data from predominantly Khasi locality of Jaiaw, we apprehended problems because of our unfamiliarity with the language and the logistics of the area. With a view to establish rapport with the respondents and the locality, we had to seek help from many 'knowledgeable' local residents, who happily accompanied us on numerous occasions, when we went for collecting data. Another difficulty we faced was that, from both the localities of our study, some of the respondents mistook us to be a salesman of some commercial goods and showed us away from their doors. But our persistent knocking at their doors made them to re-consider their appraisal of us and, at last, many of otherwise non co-operative respondents helped us to get the required data. However, it provided us with an insight in the working of the mind of the Shillongites. At the end, we have no hesitation in recording our limitation in communicating effectively through the medium of Khasi language.

In this opening chapter we have discussed the urban phenomena, urbanization in India and urban scenario in North-East and highlighted the trends of urbanization in

India. We have also tried to survey briefly the tradition of urban studies in India and abroad. The chapter ends with the objectives and methods of the present study. We propose to provide a descriptive analysis of historical setting of Shillong in the next chapter.

2

HISTORICAL SETTING OF SHILLONG

We have heavily depended for historical data required for this chapter on Shillong Centenary Celebration Souvenir (1970), B. B. Goswamy's, 'Cultural pofile of Shillong' (1978), J. P. Singh's urban Land-use planning in Hill areas: A Case Study of Shillong (1980), B. Pakem's Shillong: 1971-1981 (1984), Imdad Hussain's article on Shillong: British Enclave to Tribal city (A. C. Sinha et.al., 1993), J. N. Chaudhury's Khasi Canvas (1978), and local dailies like Shillong Times and Meghalaya Guardian.

Shillong is the capital of Meghalaya at an altitude of 1561 meter above the mean sea level. On its west and south lies the Bangladesh plain, to the east the Barak valley and to the north the valley of the Brahmaputra (Assam plain). The region enjoys a sub-tropical monsoon climate. The amount of rainfall within the region varies, ranging from between an average 300 to 400 cm, annually. Despite its undulating topography, the rejuvenated parts of the plateau leads to quick soil formation combined with high average annual rainfall that permits thick and quick vegetal growth.

Shillong is situated in the East Khasi Hills District and is linked by National Highway No. 40 with the state capital of Assam at a distance of 103 km. In the past it was a few cluster of scattered hamlets under the jurisdiction of the Syiem of Mylliem. Since the year 1866, Shillong became the provisional headquarters of the Khasi and Jaintia Hill districts. Again in 1874, Shillong was made the capital of the Assam province. Between 1905 to 1912 Shillong was turned into summer capital of newly created province of Eastern Bengal and Assam. Since then Shillong had remained the capital of Assam. However, in 1972, Meghalaya attained its full statehood and Shillong became the capital of the state.

Legends say that in ancient times a man named "SHYLLONG" discovered a deity in the Shillong peak and, therefore, the place derived its name as "SHILLONG". Among the Khasi people many such legends are current. It has got a number of tiny tablelands sparse between small hillocks. Clear water oozes out from underground sources in several places. Besides there are some perennial rivulets flowing across the city, which provide very good habitation for men and animals. Quite a number of attractive waterfalls are located within and around the city, such as Bishop's Falls, Beadon Falls, Crinoline Falls, Sweet Falls, Spread Eagle Falls, Elephant Falls etc. The highest peak is said to be the Shillong peak with a height of 6445 ft. above mean sea level. Unlike many cities of India, the atmospheric air of Shillong remains free from dirt, soot's and smoke. Approximately the humming pine trees mix their gaseous aroma containing curative ingredients for some diseases with the gentle gales that blow through the pine-needles. Rain and showers with occasional hails are welcomed gifts of nature in automatic cleansing and washing out the dirt and dregs as well as in providing rain water for collection from the house tops by every needy person for ordinary house-hold uses. The climate is humid, healthy and salubriously agreeable throughout the year. During winter, the temperature comes below freezing point and snow-flakes and frosts appear to add to the joys and fun of the youngsters. To speculative minds, the Kaleidoscopic colour variations of the sky over heading Shillong are of absorbing interests.

The British pooled in as much resources as possible for developing and making this hill-town congenial and enjoyable to their modes of living as best as possible. The beautiful Wards Lake, Polo ground, the race-course, the Governor's residence, the link-roads connecting the neighbouring plains, patronization of the Christian European missionaries with big grants of lands etc., of the establishment of quality hospitals, schools and colleges, churches and so forth are some of the good instances. They could easily discover and imagine with their world-wide experiences that Shillong was a potential virgin soil to model it into a QUEEN OF THE HILL-STATIONS on the one hand and their best strong hold in the EAST-INDIA for propagation of British power and culture. In such criss-cross pulls, anyhow Shillong has become the cleanliest, both naturally and artistically modernized, QUEEN of the cities of India.

A BRIEF BACKGROUND OF SHILLONG

An analysis of the ecological setting and patterns of the landuse reveals that the ecological conditions are not very favourable for generation of agricultural surplus. The available area for cultivation and the actually cultivated area constitute only a negligible proportion of the total geographical area. The technique of cultivation as well as the cropping pattern too indicate a highly subsistent nature of agricultural production barring a few areas of notable exception, particularly adjacent to the town. The region has some important natural resources, the forest resource being the most significant. Some amount of coal, lime-stone, sillimanite and clay is also available in some areas. But there is hardly any evidence of industries linked to such resources. The structure of the work force in the state shows little diversification with more than 80 percent of the work force concentrated in the agrarian sector alone. The development of the rural wage market too is negligible. Broadly speaking, the region, by and large, is characterized by traditional agricultural practices. There is very little evidence of any structural transformation necessitating the development of a large city. The growth of the city and its enormous size bears little symbolic relationship to the rural areas around it.

The city may be envisaged as having an enclave character, a common feature of most cities developed in the hands of colonial administration. The city sustains itself without having to depend on the structural requirement of the region. The cities developed a dependent relationship with the national / global economy and establish similar relationship with its hinterland. Shillong emerged to suit the colonial demands of exploitation of natural resources and for better administrative and defense control over the region. The regional structure, during the period of inception of the city is characterized by fragmentation of space only on politico-administrative line, without any indication towards structural changes in the economy. It is significant that the city which remained under direct British control was surrounded by numerous Khasi Himas, 'states'. Even after independence, the nature of urbanization is characterized by mere growth in the population without affecting the economic transformation of the hinterland in any significant manner.

As far as the implication of the urban growth in Meghalaya is concerned, it may be pointed out that the process of reorganization of space was externally induced leading to complete split in space linked to the national and global economy on the one hand and the hinterland continuing with the economic structure of an essentially tribal social order. The process of under development of the region thus began with this split. This was due to the reorganization of space in the region, which was not a response to changes in the regional structure through socio-economical instrumentalities. Moreover, the hegemonic and dominant character of the city space in relation to its hinterland was inherent in the process and it contributed weak linkages it had with the hinterland. Even after independence, though the city snapped its direct relationship with the metropolitan economy in the dependence structure, it continues to reproduce the process of under development by perpetuating administrative dominance.

Shillong's present economic base indicates that consequent upon its development as an administrative centre, the city has functions primarily oriented towards administration, trade and other associated roles. Concentration and growth of population has led to the growth of trade as an important function. Through administration and trade, the city has been able to develop only tertiary linkages with the rural areas in the hinterland. As a corollary the city has attracted other tertiary functions, such as concentration of banking services, educational institutions etc. resulting in to a overwhelming segment of the working force in tertiary occupation, thereby reflecting the nature of function the city is performing. The location of many state government headquarters and nearly all Central Government institutions and offices has contributed to the tertiarisation of the city's economic base. The work force in the secondary section is negligible. The production of the city is mainly geared towards meeting the consumption within the city. The production base of the city bears very little evidence of its fulfilling the requirements expected to be generated in the hinterland.

It may be mentioned that the spatial differentiation in the hilly region, which began with the dependent colonial economy, has produced the city in response to the national space economy to which it is subservient. Urbanization in the region, therefore, is more as a result of superimposed conditions, than that of indigenous growth. Within this framework the specific characteristics of the city may be underlined as follows:

1. The city is located in a hilly terrain and enjoys temperate weather conditions throughout the year, but winter months are very severe. The topography and the weather conditions not permit surplus agricultural growth.
2. The city has grown in the midst of tribal areas which continue to remain under quasi-subsistent and quasi-foraging economic organization and there is no industrial base, or production unit.
3. A very high proportion of the urban population is located in Shillong city only and the city continues to be the nodal point of all secondary and tertiary activities. The work force structure shows a heavy dependence on the tertiary and secondary sectors.
4. The city also supports a sizeable proportion of people of non-tribal origin, most of them being displaced Bengali and migrant Nepalis and Bihari population.
5. The population composition presents a high degree of ethnic diversity and economic disparities across and within varied ethnic segment.

SEARCH FOR A COLONIAL 'STATION'

During the first quarter of nineteenth century the British East India Company felt threat to its possession of Sylhet and Goalpara, its eastern frontier. Although the question of permanent British annexation of North East India was not decided as yet, David Scott, the first Civil Commissioner and Agent to the Governor-General on the North East Frontier, anticipated the future British commercial prospect in the hills. Fired by the imagination of constructing a line of communication from Rani near Palasbari in Kamrup district of Assam via Nongkhlaw. Maphlang with Sohra, bringing Brahmaputra valley nearer to Surma valley he proposed a road alignment. Accompanied by Major White, David Scott went to Nongkhlaw on 1st November 1826 and got permission from the Khasis for the construction of the road through their territory in exchange of some land in Kamrup district. Some land was granted for the construction at Nongkhlaw, of houses by the British on the terms of 1833 treaty with the Nongkhlaw Syiem, a British political officer with adequate force was posted first at Nongkhlaw. A jail was constructed earlier at Nongkhlaw. At the conclusion of Khasi Wars, Nongkhlaw, the seat of Khasi national resistance, became the first political Head Quarter of the British in the Khasi Hills. However, this Head Quarter had to be shifted to Sohra for administrative and political reasons.

There was no lime stone east of Rajmahal hills in Bihar for making lime for building construction. So the lure of lime stone brought the different warring Europeans, the British, French, Portuguese, Greeks and the Armenians to the Khasi Hills. Henry Inglish & Co. with their office at Sylhet had wide spread lime stone business interest and established themselves at least 30 years before the East India Company took up their position in the Khasi Hills. With the transfer of office of the British Political Officer from Nongkhlaw to Sohra in 1834-35, the Government ordered the removal of European detachment and abolition of convalescent depot in Sohra in view of unfavourable humid climate. W. J. Allen, Member, Board of Revenue, on deputation to Khasi Hills recommended the removal of the District headquarters to what is known today as Upper Shillong or to any situation in its vicinity.

Sohra was not considered centrally located for strategic purpose. Its transport and communication line proved inadequate during Jaintia uprising in 1860-61. Henry Hopkinson, the commissioner of Assam, took up the cause for early shifting of the District Head Quarters of Khasi Hills from Sohra to Shillong, for it was more central. It was surrounded by populous villages, whereas Sohra is in the "midst of a desert" interrupting communication at any season of the year.

Capt. E. A. Rowlatt, the Deputy Commissioner of Khasi & Jaintia Hills was asked in 1861 to submit a map of his district with a statement of population, area and the supposed height of each area above the sea level as accurately as possible. He was soon asked to proceed and make Shillong (present day Upper Shillong) his Headquarters and a small cottage was constructed there. But till early 1862, the final order of the Government of Bengal did not reach the Commissioner of Assam about the Shillong scheme. The Committee which was appointed in 1862 to select a suitable site for the District Headquarter suggested the location of it and the sanitarium of the high plateau of Shillong and to reserve the valley of Iewduh for a depot for the sick, European troops and for the cantonment. The Shillong plateau is about 275 meters higher than Iewduh with a perceptible difference in temperature. Despite the recommendation of the Site Selection Committee, the Government of Bengal ordered the shifting of Suddar Station of the District of Khasi & Jaintia Hills from Sohra to the Valley of Iewduh. A more detailed survey of Shillong and Iewduh then made by Mr. Barclay was called for and topographical survey department was asked to do it. Meanwhile a large number of people urged upon Col. Hopkinson, the Commissioner of Assam and Maj. H. S. Bivar, the Deputy Commissioner of Khasi and Jaintia Hills to give them sites for building purpose at Iewduh. In anticipation of the approval of the Government of India, the Bengal Government sanctioned the cash purchase and other arrangements, which Col. Hopkinson had made at an expenditure of Rs. 8,433/- for acquiring 2499 acres of land for the station of Shillong.

Col. Houghton was in charge of defining the area

allotments and the Commissioner of Assam, Col. Hopkinson suggested the prevailing rate at Murree Hill Station in North West Frontier of India, now Pakistan at Rs. 50/- per acre, which remained in force till 1889. Jungles were cut, some allotments were made to European and Eurasians in the core areas. Most of the migrant business people were allotted land in what is now today known as Police Bazar. Slowly the station was taking shape. But the Suddar Station of the Khasi & Jaintia Hills had not been shifted from Sohra to Iewduh as the masonry structures of the Cutchery Court was not ready to receive public offices, particularly the Treasury. Soon after the visit of Sir Cecil Beadon, the Lt. Governor of Bengal in August 1865, the construction began in right earnest. The structures were all made of stone.

On the 28 April 1866, Commissioner of Assam, Col. Henry Hopkinson, wrote to the Bengal Government, "Shillong for Yoedo. I will as well drop the name Yoedo which is quite a misapplication to the new Station and it is likely to produce confusion". Soon after the birth of Shillong, the Head Quarters of the Frontier troops, Head Quarters of the Superintending Engineer, Assam and office of Deputy Inspector General of Police, Assam were also shifted to the new district Head Quarter. The office of the Deputy Commissioner of Khasi and Jaintia Hills along with those employed in court at Sohra were transferred to Shillong. Krishna Kishor Dhar was the chief official of the Deputy commissioner's court, first at Sohra, and then at Shillong. Almost all the employees, 27 in number were persons from Sylhet.

Col. Hopkinson began to spend a considerable time at his dream town of Shillong. His presence accelerated the growth of the town. He excavated a pond with spring near the D. C's office which came to be known as Hopkinson's tank, a source of drinking water for many. It was renamed as Ward's Lake after Sir William E. Ward, who held the office of Chief Commissioner, Assam for four times at different periods between 1891 and 1896.

SHILLONG AS THE CAPITAL OF BRITISH ASSAM

Col Hopkinson in April 1867 pleaded for the location of

the Headquarters of the Assam Commission at Shillong on political, strategic and climatic ground. But the Bengal Board of Revenue regarded Shillong simply as a mere "peaked ridge", having a pleasant cool climate, which might fit it to become a sanatorium. The notion of a hill station was detrimental to the location of the Headquarters. The Governor-General in Council decided that the hill stations – Darjeeling, Sohra and Shillong were inconveniently placed as regards their accessibility to the people of the plains. The matter remained there till 1874, when Government of India constituted Assam into a Chief Commissionership directly subordinate to it. For the first 40 days the Headquarters of the Commissioner remained at Guwahati. On 20th march 1874, the Secretariat was transferred from Guwahati to Shillong for 5 reasons: climatic, political, economic, communication and strategic. Meanwhile Major S.T. Trivor, Secretary, P.W.D. Assam, in anticipation of the sanction of the Supreme Government, purchased from Col. H. S. Bivar for Rs 26,000/- a house and ground at Shillong to be used as the official residence of the Chief Commissioner, which subsequently developed into present day Raj Bhavan. Lord Northbrook was the first Governor General to visit Shillong, accompanied by the Home Secretary, Alfred C. Lyall, in August 1874.

Since then Shillong never ceased to be the capital except for a brief period. Although Assam was united with Eastern Bengal to form a new Province with Dhaka as its capital, except for a few months of 1911-12, most of the Government offices remained in Shillong during this period of 1905-1912. After 31 years of life, the Chief Commissionership of Assam lost its separate identity on 16 October 1905. The phased transfer of capital to Dhaka was spread over five years. The homecoming from Dhaka to Shillong in 1912 did not take much time.

Shillong was an artifact of the British rule, created for administrative purpose, almost out of nothing. Jungles were cleared, roads laid, houses constructed and offices built for administrative purpose. The town had not sprung up on a natural trade route. It became an administrative centre rather than a commercial outpost. With the shifting of the offices from Sohra to Shillong, came from there a few eminent muslim businessmen hailing from Bengal, who bought property in and around Police Bazar. Golan Haidara, Haji Kasimuddin Molla, Moula Box, Zamatulla, Abdul Gaffar and Saikh Dedar Box contributed much to commercial, religious and social life of early days of Shillong.

By 1878, the British Shillong had 106 house holdings in Thana Road, Jail Road, European ward and a population of 2155 people. An officially nominated Municipal Board was set up and Syiem of Mylliem, Hain Manick, was also a nominated member of the Board. Munshi Md. Ahsanulla was nominatcd on 24 February, 1879 and continued till 1894. Shillong, an official town had no water works and street light. The water supply scheme of Shillong was completed in 1883-84. By 1895, Rev. J. C. Evans, Kartik Chandra Chatterjee and Saday Charan Das were nominated to the Municpal Board, which got jurisdiction by this time over European Ward, Laban, Mawkhar, Civil or Police Bazar and Jail Road Quarters.

With the formation of Chief Commissionership of Assam in 1874, came from Guwahati, 33 officials of all categories from head assistant to sweeper, who formed the nucleus of newly organised Secretariat. Most of them got accommodation in Jail Road and Thana Road residential sites and some at Laban, outside the limits of British territory. Shillong covered during the British days, both British and non-British territory. Out of 10 square kilometers of Shillong, 4 square kilometers were British territory and was the only instance, when core employees of a capital of a British Province was in non-British territory. As the Secretariat was in British territory, this did not create any administrative problem. The Station consisted of land either ceded by the Syiem of Mylliem or leased by private parties and areas allowed from time to time by the Syiem of Mylliem.

Social and religious institutions were coming up at Shillong with the transfer of District head quarters from Sohra to Shillong. Bengali Muslim businessmen in the Civil Bazar established soon the Police Bazar Masjid at the entrance of Thana Road on a site donated by Golan Haidar. Anglican Church services were conducted under official patronage at the Government House in 1875 and prior to that in a room in the Cutchery for quite some time till the All Saints Cathedral was built in 1876. It was razed to the ground by the great earthquake and subsequently rebuilt in 1902. Calvinistic Protestant Church under Welsh Mission came in Mawkhar village at the edge of the administrative town of Shillong. The first church was opened in 1874 in Mawkhar and rebuilt in 1886. The Catholic Church came to Shillong with the German Salvatorians under Father Otto Hopfenmuller on 27 February, 1890. At that time there were hardly 20 European and Anglo Indian Catholics in Shillong. With the coming of Father Christopher Becker in march 1906, the Catholic Church spread in Shillong particularly in Laitumkhrah village. The Unitarian was born in Jowai in 1887. It came to Shillong at Madan Laban and was consolidated by Dr. J. Thomas Sunderland, who came from U. K. in 1896.

Outside the British territory of Shillong in Laban, in 1896 Laban Sanatan Dharma Sabha (Laban Hari Sabha) was established under the presidentship of Rai Saheb Prasanna Kumar Bhattacharjee, assisted by Surendro Kumar Chakraborty and Joy Govinda Choudhury. At the heart of British Shillong in Thana Road in 1901. Shillong Hindu Dharma Sabha (Jagannath Mandir) came up on a rent-free leaseland. With the shifting of the District Head Quarters from Sohra to Shillong, Raj Chandra Choudhury and Brojendra Nath Sen brought Brahmo Samaj to Shillong. A Mahila Samiti and Ram Mohan Library were started in 1887 by Hemanta Kumari Choudhury in Jail Road. Later on it was shifted to Laban. Khasi Hills Brahmo Samaj mandir was built up in Laban in 1904 on a plot of land donated by Raj Chandra Choudhury. Nilmoni Chakraborty, a Brahmo preacher, was sent by Sib Nath Shastri. Nilmoni Chakraborty left Shillong in 1889 for Sohra and made Brahmo Samaj movement a village reconstruction programme supported by Dr. Hem Chandra Wallang and by Prakash Chandra Pal. Some Bengali Brahmos mostly hailing from Guwahati and Calcutta established Shillong Brahmo Samaj at Police Bazar in 1874. They built their Mandir at Police Bazar in 1878. The Brahmo Samaj movement in Shillong was confined mostly to upper class Bengali officials, a few Khasis and a few Assamese. Babu Jebon Roy was a friend of the Brahmos.

The Chief Commissioner of Assam did not take any initiative to provide education to European and Anglo Indian children. On the direction of Government of India, the Assam administration opened European and Eurasian girls boarding and day school at Shillong in March 1881 under the management of the chaplain of Shillong. It was closed down and private initiative was encouraged from 1888. The administration encouraged Miss Blake's Shillong Mixed School for the middle class European and Eurasian children. This school was closed down in 1896 and the Government had to open a school under the supervision of the D. P. I., Assam, near Laban on the old site after the great earthquake of June 1896. It grew up as Pine Mount School for girls. There was a church of England Boarding School for girls just over the Golf Club ground.

The Jail Road infant school started in a hut constructed by the Jail Road Society Hall Committee, which got the land from the Deputy Commissioner. Lt. Col. Howell in 1896 donated by the Government for social and religious purposes. The lease was granted on the same terms on which Shillong Club and Shillong Uncovenented Service Club were granted, their holdings in August 1894 and in October 1896 respectively. The land was in an unsanitary and dangerous condition, when it was given by Lt. Col. Howell. It was improved by the Jail Road Society Hall Committee. A hall was erected for public and religious purposes such as Durga Puja and Saraswati Puja. The hall was used for a Sunday school and for an infant school. Rai Bahadur S. C. Das, was the President of the Committee and Chandra Nath Sarma its secretary. Rai Saheb Mohendra Chandra Dutta, Raj Kumar Nandi, Dakshina Ch. Nandi, Girish Chandra Chakravorty, Sarada Charan Dhar, Prasanna Kumar Dutta and Prasanna Kumar Choudhuri were other leading members.

Babu Jeebon Roy, born in 1838, founded Shillong Zillah High School in 1875-76. His son, Sib Charan Roy, passed the entrance examination from this school in 1880 from its Sylhet centre. After a decade, it was taken over by Assam government and came to be known as Shillong Government Boys High School. Rev. J. C. Evans was appointed

Headmaster in 1891. Khasi Jaintia Presbyterian Girls High School was established by the Welsh Mission in 1892. Ms. Bossin William was its Principal till 1896. Jeebon Roy also started Mawkhar Bengali School for Khasi boys and ran it for a few decades. Shillong Bengali Girls School was established in 1883 as a primary school but eventually was raised to Middle Vernacular school level. Prasanna Kumar Bose was its secretary in 1902 and Dinanath Dhar took it over in 1903.

A terrible earthquake occurred in Shillong on 12 June 1897. All masonry buildings including the Government House, Secretariat, church, jail, public offices and private houses were levelled to the ground. All services including Tonga service to Guwahati of M/s Golan Hyder and Sons were disrupted and so also the Shillong water works. The Deputy Commissioner, F. C. Arbuthnott, was fired by the imagination of bringing railways to Upper Shillong, from Sylhet making it the new capital. A scheme was on foot for a railway to Nongjuri and Shella at the foothills and its ultimate connection to Shillong via Laitlyngkot. One can still see the abandoned railway track on a way to Shella village. But the successive Chief Commissioners, Sir Henry John Stedman Cotton and Sir W. E. Ward were against it for financial reasons. Reconstruction of the city began on old sites.

Even after the earthquake, the reconstructed Assam Secretariat was small enough to be located in a single building in the Secretariat Hill. In 1874, the Public Works Department Secretariat was also located there. This arrangement made for single method of intercommunication between the departments of the Secretariat. Nanda Kishore Dhar, the Head Assistant was called the father of Secretariat. Most of the civil secretariat employees were Bengalis of Sylhet. Among the Assamese, Maulavi Peer Buksh, held the Chief Ministerial appointment and exercised greater deal of influence. The Head Assistant in the general department was the highest paid ministerial officer in the civil secretariat till 1880. Md. Peer Buksh was appointed as the Superintendent of Assam Secretariat (P. W. D.) in 1886. Prakash Chandra Deb, was the first Bengali to become the Superintendent on the retirement of E. Harrison in 1891 in Assam Secretariat (civil).

Sarat Chandra Dhar succeeded Prakash Chandra Deb as the superintendent (civil) in 1897. On his retirement, Charu Chandra Goswami was appointed to this office in 1904. In 1906, in the Eastern Bengal and Assam Secretariat, the post was upgraded with higher supervisory power and Charu Chandra Goswami became the first Registrar in 1906, who formed the vital link between the government and the establishment. He was in charge of whole of the Secretariat staff. From time to time, the Registrars performed the duties of the under secretariat as well. The great Registrar, Mahendra Kumar Gupta officiated as under secretary in 1919.

During the period 1864-1915, the core sector of Shillong became and remained non-tribal, essentially Bengali. Like the core town, the composition of Shillong remained undesigned. Shillong was the British creation for administrative and strategic reasons. With the arrival of those who were employed at the office of the Deputy Commissioner at Sohra and with the shifting of the business establishments, mostly Bengali Muslims, who were doing well at Sohra and more so, with the formation of Chief Commissionership of Assam in 1874, came from Guwahati 33 officials of all categories from Head Assistant to Sweepers, who formed the nucleus of newly organised Assam Secretariat. The official town had overwhelmingly a Bengali flavour. It was a historical accident. The neighbouring village of Laban and Mawkhar had Khasi composition. A few Bengali families, with permission of the Syiem of Mylliem settled down in Laban village.

In 1878, at the time of the formation of the Municipal Board, the core town of Shillong had a population of 2,149. In 1881, there were 4288 persons in the town and in the next decade the population increased to 6,720. In 1901, Shillong had a population of 9,621. It increased to 13,639 in 1911. In 1894, the ministerial composition in the Assam Secretariat was Bengali with a few Assamese and very few Khasis. In 1914, the Assam Secretariat establishment had more Bengali Hindus than Assamese, Muslims or Khasis. The main point is that there were not sufficient number of Assamese or Khasi clerks in the Secretariat. In 1914, the

Secretariat establishment was composed of 43 Bengali Hindus, 5 Muslims, 10 Khasis and 8 others. The office, as it stood in 1915, was transferred wholesale from Dhaka to Shillong after reformation of Assam in 1912. The Assamese were reluctant to leave their valley for service in Shillong. The Secretariat hardly got an entrance or an F. A. passed Khasi on Rs. 50/- per month. But with the spread of education, the position changed in the Secretariat. The number of Khasis rose to 13 in permanent category and 3 as temporary by 1917. However, very few of them lived in the core town.

All together Shillong grew without any plan. The growth of the town had been lopsided on an adhoc basis. There was an acute absence of long term strategy in the growth. Frontier administration stamp continued on its face. Those brave men, who came and lived in Shillong, had very little comfort and convenience of human being. In the first phase they lived and worked in small, ill-ventilated asymetric stone houses and after the great earthquake of 1897, small Assam type structures of wood and reed walls with corrugated iron sheet roofs, dark, dingy and ill ventilated mushroomed. There was no electricity. They were not big persons nor were they highly educated, most of them passed entrance examination for Fine Arts. The dynamics of social and political development did not touch the hills in the early days of Shillong. Those brave men and women who lived there had some commitment. It was an official town. It became in its early years clerk-oriented which had limited vision. There was a distressing shortage of high officers with social commitment. They had little concern for the small men's hardship, difficulties, hopes and aspiration.

At this moment of despondency in April 1901, Swami Vivekananda came to Shillong. He inaugurated the newly constructed Quinton Hall and gave a clarion call in the meeting presided over by the Chief Commissioner of Assam, Sir Henry Cotton on 27 April 1901 which was reported in U Khasi Mynta (May 1901). Swami preached new humanism as universal religion, the essence of which being service to humanity, help to the poor and spread of education in the society.

DEVELOPMENT OF MUNICIPAL GOVERNMENT

Shillong had no local Government for more than decades after its annexation by the British. There was not even a town improvement committee, which existed in the plain districts of Assam. It was in 1878, that initiative was taken by the government for the introduction of local self-government in Shillong. The government suggested to the Deputy commissioner, Khasi and Jaintia Hills, that Shillong might be constituted into a municipality. The latter thought that it might be constituted into a union and not a municipality. Later on, however, the Deputy Commissioner agreed with the Government that Shillong might be constituted into a 'Station'. The Chief Commissioner agreed with the proposal and directed the Deputy Commissioner to take necessary measures in that direction. In the meanwhile a petition was submitted to the Deputy Commissioner requesting him the inclusion of Mawkhar and Laban within the jurisdiction of the proposed station. But these two areas were not within the British territory. They were under the control of the Syiem of Mylliem, and therefore, there was some difficulty in the extension of the Municipal Act of 1976 to these areas. At the same time the Deputy Commissioner came to the conclusion that these two areas mus^t be brought under Municipal control. Otherwise, there would be no improvement in the sanitation of the localities. The Deputy Commissioner did not contemplate, the inclusion of Mawkhar and Laban within the jurisdiction of the Shillong Station. He was sure that the Syiem of Mylliem, who controlled these areas, would carry out the instruction given to him. While agreeing with the Deputy Commissioner that the inclusion of these two areas within the jurisdiction of Shillong Station would be objectionable, the Government requested him to suggest the steps that ought to be taken for their inclusion. The Deputy Commissioner, without the consent of the Syiem of Mylliem issued a declaration including these two areas in the proposed 'Station'. The Syiem of Mylliem protested. He promised to improve the sanitary condition of these two villages. The Deputy Commissioner, gently persuaded the Syiem with a small bribe the Commissionership of the Station Committee – to agree to the inclusion of Mawkhar and Laban within the Shillong Station. The Syiem consented and agreed to pay on behalf of the residents of these two villages, the rates levied by the Station Committee and do anything and everything required by the Deputy Commissioner, provided his ownership and authority were not undermined.

On 26th November 1878, a proclamation was issued constituting Shillong, and its suburbs, Laban and Mawkhar into a Station. Thus, to begin with, the administrative area of the Shillong Station was limited to the British territory of Shillong plus Laban and Mawkhar. Lachumiere was not a part of the Shillong Station. But the Assam-Bengal Railway Company, located in Lachumiere, was taking water free from the Municipal water supply system, with the permission of Col. Grey, the Deputy Commissioner of the Khasi and Jaintia Hills. Arbuthnott, his successor, thought that the company was not entitled to take water free from the Municipal water supply system. The situation was delicate because he had to interfere with the decision of his predecessor. To obviate this difficult situation, Arbuthnott proposed the inclusion of Lachumiere into the Shillong Station so that the company might be taxed for taking water. But the Syiem of Mylliem objected the inclusion of Lachumiere in the ground that it was close to his villages of Malki and Laitumkhrah. Later on, he agreed to the proposal and Lachumiere was included within the Shillong Station.

There was further extension of the administrative area of the Shillong Municipality. In 1905, the village, Heneng Umkhrah was included into the Municipality, because the clerks transferred from East Bengal were residing there and utilizing Municipal services. Further, the place became unsanitary because of the congregation of many people there. In 1906, the Government suggested to the Station Committee the inclusion of Nongthymmai as a part of the Shillong Station, but the committee did not accept the suggestion. Later on Nongthymmai was included in the Shillong Station.

In 1910, the Government decided to include the areas between Umshyrpi and Umkhrah rivers near about Shillong within the Municipal limits of Shillong Station. This was done in consultation with the Syiem of Mylliem, who controlled the territory. The Syiem called for a Durbar of Mantris, which laid down certain conditions and the Government of Assam accepted them.

Shillong Municipality

On 20th March 1909, the Shillong Station Committee resolved that it might be converted into a municipality. The officiating Commissioner of the Surma Valley was not wholly in favour of the proposal. He wrote to the Government:

> "I have already indicated that the conversion of the station into a municipality is not without drawbacks. Shillong is the headquarter of the Government and it appears to me highly necessary that the Government should insist on the management of the place being kept at a higher standard, which I am afraid is very rarely maintained in the average municipality of the province. It is absolutely essential that the Lt. Governor should have the power to step in and veto proposals of the municipal board or compel them to carry out necessary works. Inefficient and insanitary management would be intolerable at a place, which is at once a health resort, and the summer headquarter of the Government. Every conceivable precaution must be taken to maintain and safeguard the authority, which is now and must always be exercised by the executive government. In the first place, Shillong should undoubtedly be notified a town of which the Commissioners as well as the chairman are nominated by the local government. It is worthy of note that in Bengal, Darjeeling falls within this category".

The Government accepted the proposal. The station was converted into a Municipality in December 1910. The Government requested the Commissioner of the Surma valley to nominate a person for appointment as chairman. The Commissioner nominated the Deputy Commissioner of the Khasi and Jaintia Hills and he was appointed Chairman of the Board for the first time.

SHILLONG AS AN ADMINISTRATIVE CENTRE

Until independence was achieved and sometime after that Shillong retained its character of small but important administrative outpost along with that of a less frequented and so quiet and lovely hill-station. It was sheltered from the movements that agitated the plains and the roads to it being easily controllable with check gates and any political unrest could be stopped from penetrating here. Indeed popular leaders did raise their voice against the location beyond the reach of the common man in the plains, yet they retained Shillong as the capital after independence, but decided to change its restricted character by a process of induction, introducing more of elements of the state. Accordingly, large areas around the nucleus available after the partition of the country and the departure of a large number of British owners, were procured where Government employees from the plains were given lands on loan to be recouped in easy installments. This led to the rapid growth of the "Shillong Urban Agglomeration", because with the sudden growth of the administrative structure to deal with the new commitments of the welfare state, housing problems had grown acute and the owners of houses could earn good income in rent. There were only 17 Government quarters in 1949 for the clerks. The small defense set-up also expanded. A number of the Central Government surveys like the Anthropological, Botanical, Zoological, Geological etc, established their regional offices here and all these put tremendous pressure on the limited housing accommodation both for the offices and their personnel. The rapid growth of the various administrative set-up led to the expansion of the market and trading institutions and traders. All these together raised rents and the office personnel gladly availed of the offer of the Government of Assam to own their own houses at the state expense and thereby adding to their income from salaries. This resulted in the growth of 'colonies' of the people from the plains – outside the core town in the theory, but within it in reality of these the new colonies were mostly of the Brahmaputra valley, only one being of tribal groups from other hills. A large number of persons displaced from East Bengal were also settled in two major concentrations. The local people, however, were not interested at the beginning in the housing and settlement schemes as they already had their own residence and lands. The tempo of expansion slowly, however, pushed them out of the heart of the township. A return drive for holdings within greater Shillong is a recent phenomenon as the consequence of growth of urbanization and availability of ready money as compensation for the lands acquired for the Barapani project.

The development of Shillong with that of the administration there created three layers or rings which reflect the chronology of the process – the oldest town is Bengali, the post-Independent Assamese and the last the Khasi with another big section would be the growing defence personnel as defence is a rapidly growing organization here. A sprinkling of Mizo is noticeable in the last belt.

Thc manner of growth and Shillong being the capital of a multi-ethnic, multi-cultural and multi-linguistic state brought together mainly through government services has created a confederal type of association in which different groups have kept themselves socially separate mixing only in their official and trade purposes. English, is the upper level and Hindi in the lower are the links of inter-communication. The status of the British administrators had set the style of the urban culture which continues to be European in form.

Shillong has a start over other capitals in the region. It has an administrative tradition and establishment, whereas Gauhati had to start afresh. Arunachal Pradesh has yet to build its headquarters, Agartala, Imphal and Kohima are yet to attain administrative eminence already achieved by Shillong. Still Shillong has to be primarily an administrative centre – for a state, for a district, for district council and for a number of the Central Government and defence organizations.

The present panoramic pinewood view of the town does not seem to have been in existence in the early sixties of the nineteenth century. It then looked as if clad with jungles, the plateau of Iewduh is then said to have been mostly devoid of trees and was very sparsely populated. The bazaar at Iewduh was, however, largely attended and was considered a sacred place. As a whole, nearly all the villages in the district were mere hamlets with less than 500 inhabitants and in many to them, there were not more than 3 to 5 houses. The

1872 census report described Shillong as a sanatorium serving as a military station and headquarters of the district, but was no better than a mere bazaar and its population was too insignificant to be mentioned in the report.

Of the villages in existence by then around Shillong, Laban was worth mentioning. This is why the Khasis even today call Shillong as Laban. The other villages, viz. Mawkhar, Mawprem, Laitumkhrah, Nongthymmai and Mawlai were also said to have existed then, but had very meagre population. The valley of Laitumkhrah, Malki and Pynthorumkhrah were then largely paddy fields. As regards population of the villages, no records were available.

The real expansion of the town actually started since 1874. In 1874, by the proclamation dated the 6th February and 12th September, Assam was separated from Bengal and converted into a province under the chief Commissioner. Consisting of the districts, now forming the districts of Assam, Sylhet district of Bangladesh, Meghalaya and Nagaland. Shillong was chosen as the seat of the new administration. The foundation stone of the capital was laid down by Col. Hopkinson, the then Commissioner of Assam. Simultaneously, construction of a cart-road between Gauhati and Shillong was undertaken. The road was opened to pony-carts and bullock-carts in late 1875. During that period, the main communication between Shillong and the rest of the country was via Cherrapunjee through Sylhet. It was in 1878 that Laban and Mawkhar were brought under the Municipal control of Shillong under the Agreement No. LXIV with U Hain Manik, the Syiem of Mylliem. On 26th November 1878, a 'Station' was constituted at Shillong covering the ceded areas, Jail Road, Police Bazar and European quarters and the non-ceded suburbs, Laban and Mawkhar, under Act V (B. C) of 1876. The administration of the Station was entrusted to a committee consisting of six members, with the Deputy Commissioner as the ex-officio chairman. The committee afterwards was expanded to twelve members, five of the members held their seats by virtue of their official status and the remaining seven were nominated by the Chief Commissioner.

In the 1881 census, Shillong recorded 4,288 persons, including those stationed in the cantonment. The population of the civil station alone was 3,737 and were broadly classified into the following religious groups - Hindu, 1,862 (49.83 percent), Muslim - 311 (8.32 percent) and others - 1,564 (41.85 percent). From the percentage distribution of other major religions in Shillong for the year (Census of India 1881) and that of 1891, it can safely be inferred that 1,564 persons in the other groups in 1881 consisted chiefly of Christians and animists. In 1891, 6,720 inhabitants were enumerated in Shillong together with the cantonment (810:12.05 percent), and increase of 56.7 percent during the last decade. As per census records, the population consisted mainly of Government officials, traders and others.

The devastating earthquake of 1897 retarded the growth of Shillong to a great extent. It levelled to the ground almost all masonry structures in no time. It was followed by incessant rain, dysentery and fever during the latter half of 1897 and during 1898 and 1899. Since 1897, all the buildings have been constructed in Shillong of timber, reeds and plaster to get rid of the severity of the earthquake. The construction activities was greatly intensified and so absorbed more and more persons in it. The population of Shillong, therefore, shot up to 9,621 in 1901, an increase of 2,901 persons (43.2 percent) over 1891.

In 1905, the province of Eastern Bengal and Assam, now defunct, was created under a Lt. Governor, and Shillong was made the temporary headquarter of the administration. This necessitated the expansion of the offices and creation of many more new departments, resulting in the increase of population and dwellings. As a result, the existing localities became dense and new localities sprang up. Thus, the history of Shillong tells us that before the administrative headquarters was started in 1866, the area, where the town now stands, was sparsely inhabited, but there were a few villages on the lower slopes of the Shillong peak besides Iewduh, the largest weekly market in the district. The selection of Shillong as the new district head quarter by the committee set up in 1864 is now a matter of history as well as the subsequent decision to build the 'civil station' on the slopes of Iewduh instead of the original decision to locate it on the slopes of the Shillong peak itself.

The civil station was started between the then existing Khasi villages of Mawkhar and Laitumkhrah which became as these were satellites of the new administrative head quarters. In 1874, when Sir Robert Campbell was Lieutenant General of Bengal, Assam was separated from Bengal and Shillong became the head quarters of the new chief Commissioner's province of Assam and the establishment of the Secretariat and office of the Heads of Departments gave further impetus to its growth. In 1874, Lord Northbrook, the Viceroy, visited Shillong. He ordered that certain tracts in the neighbourhood of the town be reserved to protect its water supply and to form a fuel reserve. This, in later years became what is known as the 'Green Belt' around the town. In 1875, however, Shillong could hardly be called a town. Its population was less than that of Shella, the largest Khasi village and less than one quarter of the population of Jowai, the sub-divisional headquarters. However, better communications with the opening of a cart road to Gauhati in 1877 hastened the growth of the town.

Although Shillong was constituted a station under Act V (B. C) 1876 in 1878 and a Town Committee was appointed which was presided over by the Deputy Commissioner, it would hardly be fair to describe it as a typical town in the 19th century. In fact, we may say that it was still a collection of villages with the administrative area in the centre and the satellite Khasi villages, like Mawkhar, Laitumkhrah and Laban located some distance away from it.

In later years, this cluster of villages developed rapidly. The partition of Bengal in 1905 and the formation of the new province of Assam and Eastern Bengal gave fresh impetus to the development of the town as the temporary headquarters of the provincial administration which ultimately shifted to Dacca in 1910. The town developed rapidly. The most remarkable development being in the "civil station" the name under which the administrative area was known in the old correspondence, as a result of the large number of new offices which came up in the town. There was a corresponding development in the satellite villages, especially Laban village where most of the Government employees chose to reside.

It would be interesting to try to obtain a glimpse of Shillong of the Victorian ear. The civil station consisted of a few Government offices, mostly on the Secretariat hill over looking the Wards Lake and the bungalows for European officials located in what was called the "European quarters" which was the area encircled by Bivar Road. Mawkhar now a crowded locality in the centre of the town was then an idyllic village with scattered cottages nestling in the shade of stately trees or huge clumps of bamboos. The village path ran through the middle of the village. This is now Mawkhar main road. Tigers, leopards and other denizens of the forest roamed the Mawkhar and Iewduh areas freely even during daylight and it was not unusual for citizens to see these animals while they went about their daily business. Col. Wilson mentioned that he shot two leopards on the same day new Iewduh (Bara Bazar) in the closing years of the last century.

With the years, the Khasi villages expanded outwards and at the same time, the civil station also underwent development. A small market was started near the police station which of late grew out of all recognition, but still retains its original name of 'Police Bazar', even by the turn of the century. Mawkhar had grown both in size and expense. The main road was being paved with boulders and out-lying areas like Riatsamthiah, Jaiaw and Mawlai had just come into existence. Laitumkhrah was another idyllic village with fields growing besides the village path which is now Laitumkhrah main road. The area was covered by jungle and tall grass where even in the late twenties wild animals roamed about freely. The last recorded tiger shot at Laitumhrah was in 1928, when a tiger visited the staff quarters of St. Edmund's college. In the thirties, new settlements came up, like Nongthymmai (New village) and 'Bhagyakul' which locally was known under the unhappy name of 'New Colony'.

The development of the town during the reign of King Edward VII received a set-back with the departure of the temporary capital from Shillong to Dacca in 1910, but with the succession of King George V, the partition of Bengal was reversed at the coronation Durbar held at Delhi in 1912. The old Chief Commissioner's province of Assam was revived with its headquarters as previously in Shillong. Since then, the town has not looked back and there has been a history of continued development which reached its highest momentum.

With the years, the surrounding villages expanded upto the limits of the civil station which itself underwent rapid development with the growth of government offices as well as the shopping area at Police Bazar. By the nineteen twenties, the pattern began to emerge and Shillong became more or less as we know it today, i.e., a mozaic composed of constituent units with the civil station at the centre and the various adjoining areas like Laban, Laïtumkhrah, etc. which were earlier its satellites, but which had now expanded right upto the civil station forming one heterogeneous entity. From the nineteen thirties, Shillong began to expand outwardly as there was no further scope for expansion internally within the constituent units.

The historical background and the development of the town cast their influence on the town we know today. Everyone of the constituent units which together form the town retains its individual character and it could be said that each of the various localities has its own unique and unmistakable characteristics.

The administrative area which was the old 'civil station' of former days is now in the centre of the town. It has become much more crowded with all the new offices set up during the past few years. The appearance of this area has also changed with time and it has now many imposing concrete buildings, which have been built during the last 20 years. The spirit however remains unchanged and the old secretariat hill, where Colonel Keatinge set up his office, is still the hub of Government activities, although with the passage of time, government offices have expanded right upto the edges of old station and in certain areas have actually spilt over into the adjoining parts of the town. The cantonment still retains much of the atmosphere it originally had since the early years of Shillong and the old bungalows continue to stand secluded in fairly large compounds.

Sitting in the lawns of these bungalows with the pine trees all around and with tall hedges shutting the compound off from the outside world, one experiences the feeling of being transported back to the old Shillong of fifty years ago, and of being far away from the din and bustle of everyday town life. Mawkhar was the oldest location outside the civil station. Here, the Syiem of Mylliem set up his office and court after the civil station was set up. With the years, the importance of the Mawkhar court and office increased while that of the Syiem's old headquarters at Mylliem village declined. The locality still retains its reputation of being the oldest part of the town and many old buildings can still be seen some of which have interesting historical associations.

Laban was from the beginning and still is mainly a residential area for government officers and other employees. Like localities inhabited by government employees all over the world, it is a quiet part of the town. This area underwent its first major development in 1905 when Shillong was made a temporary capital of the new province of Assam and Eastern Bengal for 5 years from 1905 – 1910. In 1912, the province of Assam was revived and since then government employees have settle down in this area in large numbers. The most recent addition were in the nineteen fifties when new areas like Bishnupur, etc., were opened up. In the old days, Laban was the most developed part of the town and villagers in the surrounding areas even today refer to the town as 'Laban'.

The process of growth and development continues today and Laitumkhrah which was a quiet rural area even 40 years ago, is now a crowded, busy locality in the middle of the town. Even newly opened areas, like Nongthymmai are now very much a part of the town and the town is still expanding outwards swallowing up the surrounding country side. A couple of decades ago, Mawlai, as the name implies (Maw-stone, Lai-three) was a satellite village at the third mile post on the road to Gauhati. Now the village has expanded right upto the Umkhrah stream which was once the limit of the town and year by year we see Mawlai itself expanding along the National Highway to Gauhati. It is proposed to set up Town Committee in three outlying areas which were once satellite villages but are now very much part of the town.

We find therefore, that every locality has in its own way preserved the heritage of the past. Each one of the town's localities retains its own individual character and anyone living in own part of the town would feel the change if he is to move to another part some distance away.

The administrative area in the centre of the town retains its role as the administrative centre of the State, while the older settled areas like Mawkhar and Laban have an atmosphere of what we may call age, compared to the newer areas like Laitumkhrah and the newly opened parts, show signs of unmistakable life and vigour compared to the older parts of the town. As a particular example, one may quote the continuing growth of Laitumkhrah Bazar and markets in outlying localities compared to the decline of older markets like Paltan Bazar and perhaps to some degree even Police Bazar. In this aspect the town resembles a living growth with some parts already old, while at the extremity it is showing rapid growth and putting out fresh branches.

In the modern Shillong of today, however, the past lives on in a hundred different ways. The narrow winding streets which were in many areas originally village paths and which even till the late twenties rarely saw a motor car are now crowded with traffic and traffic jams which are the nightmare of larger cities have begun to make their debut. Old roads and old buildings still stand here and there. Even thirty years ago, one could see traditional Khasi houses with thatched roofs curved like a rhino's back standing along the main roads of the town. These have now disappeared as they have been pulled down to make way for newer cottages with corrugated iron roofs, and in the later years, to reinforced concrete buildings. Occasionally however, some conservative owner has replaced the old grass roof with a tin one but retained the quaint curved shape of the original, which serves as a reminder of an almost forgotten period in the town's history. The past also lives on in institutions like the office of the headman which still continues in some localities of the town and which appears to be a hang over of the old days in that it is the continuation of the old institution of the village headman.

As the town grows, and the past recedes ever further away into oblivion, the town will develop towards a homogeneous entity that will be the city of tomorrow. But today, we are thankful for whatever remains of the heterogeneous past which has conferred on each locality of the town a distinct unique character reminiscent of its origin.

After British withdrawal from India in 1947, for the next 25 years, Shillong served as the state capital of Assam. These were the days of expectations, euphoria, frustration, agitations and training period of democratic polity. Shillong turned out to be the hub of various tribal movements for autonomy. It appears that the Assamese elite like their British predecessors failed to identify themselves with the aspirations of the hill people. Consequently, after the separation of Naga Hills District as state of Nagland in 1963, Lushai Hills District as Mizoram and NEFA as Arunachal Pradesh and Khasi and Jaintia Hills and Garo Hills Districts as Meghalaya were created as federating units of the Indian Union in 1972. Shillong turned out to be the capital of Meghalaya, instead of Assam, but in the bargain it turned out to be the regional headquarters of a number of Central government establishments. Army, Air Force, Assam Rifles, Border Security Force, various All India Surveys such as Anthropological, Botanical, Geological etc., North Eastern Hill University, North Eastern Council, various Scientific bodies like Atomic Energy Commission, Indian Council of Agricultural Research etc. all chose Shillong as their regional headquarters. These developments resulted in influx of a sizeable non-local migrants to the city.

The states were created out of the hill districts after prolonged peaceful and not so peaceful agitations. That left a sizeable segment of the tribal population in cogitation. Partition of British India into India and Pakistan had led to arrival of Bengali refugees in the region, leading to tribal, non-tribal and Bengali and Assamese conflicts. The war of liberation of Bangladesh 1971-72, created a situation in which a sizeable East Pakistanis took shelter in India in general and Meghalaya in particular. It is alleged that atleast some of the refugees never returned to Bangladesh. Since then clandestine migration of the Bangladeshis in the region and in Meghalaya in particular is on. So much so that entire Indo-Bangladesh border is being fenced with live electric wire.

Some or other form of insurgency in Nagaland has been going on since 1947. In course of time, Mizos took to arms. Since 1980s even small a section of the Assamese raised the flag of secession from the Indian Union. Manipur and Tripura had a series of rebel outfit by the last quarter of the 20th century. By the last decade of the 20th century, even the placid Garos and the Khasis began to display symptoms of unrest and a series of underground bodies began to operate in and around the city of Shillong. In this way, the obvious serenity of scenic Shillong has an under current of ethnic unrest, distorting its old image of an oasis of peace.

To sum up, the Chapter provides a brief historical survey of evolution of Shillong. It informs the readers how it was created as an administrative centre for the newly created tribal district. Within no time, its locational advantages were discerned and Shillong was turned into state capital of Assam for the next hundred years. Side by side, its merit as a health resort and cantonment for the armed forces, was key consideration for the British. After independence of India, Shillong began to play an increasing role in the regional context as the metropolitan centre for various forums. At the end, we have noted how Shillong did not remain untouched from various shades of ethnic migration and movements. The next chapter analyses the development of the ethnic mozaic of the city and its aftermath.

3

ETHNIC MOSAIC

The urban community is neither an undifferentiated mass nor a haphazard collection of buildings and people. In the residential differentiation of the city the fabric comes to resemble a 'mosaic of social worlds' (Wirth, 1938). Similar populations cluster together and come to characterize their areas. As Robert Park puts it: "In the course of time every sector and quarter of the city takes on something of the character and qualities of its inhabitants". Each separate part of the city is inevitably stained with the peculiar sentiments of its population. The effect of this is to convert what was at first a mere geographical expression into a neighbourhood, that is to say, a locality with sentiments, traditions, and a history of its own" (Park, 1952).

The residential differentiation of the urban population takes place in terms of many attributes and in many ways. Almost any criterion which can be used for differentiating between individuals and groups may become the basis for their physical separation. The process of separation may be accomplished through force, through a variety of sanctions, through a voluntary aggregation designed as a defense against unfamiliar ideas or customs or as an escape from persecution and discrimination, and through a selection of market forces (Johnson, 1943). In much early town planning residential differentiation and segregation appear as prime characteristics. In town plans by Diirer and Fiirtenbach different crafts or guilds are allocated different blocks and a rough zonation in terms of wealth is envisaged (Dickinson, 1951). In many towns of medieval Europe, and more recently in those of much of Asia and North Africa, the urban fabric is physically divided into wards and quarters. Descriptions of the characteristics of life in the various quarters form a favourite literary enterprise (Mumford, 1961). The place of quarters in the ecological structure of Arab cities is described by Baer, "old districts, and even more so, the old city, are divided into quarters. In the old city they are fairly secluded from one another. The number of entrances to the quarter is small, and each has a gate which may be shut, and sometimes is, even in these days. The quarter was an independent unit until recently (and in some cities still is), with its own mukhtar... religious functionary, night-watchman, etc... In the not so distant past, there used to be disputes and sometimes actual fights between groups of youths belonging to different parts of the city. In many cities there used to be much segregration of religious sects by quarter, and in some parts this remains the case... perhaps even more commonly, members of a single linguistic or national group live together in a quarter"(Baer, 1966).

A similar theme is reported about cities South of the Sahara, in Africa: "In some parts of the West African territories ... members of tribes other than the dominant one live customarily in separate parts of the town.... Within a distinct administrative unit with its own chief and elders"(UNESCO, 1957). In Japan, Yazaki remarks that the division of the ancient castle town 'were planned by the ruler and each section of the city was occupied exclusively by members of a particular status group. Not only was the style of residences altered in the different status area, but the mode of administration differed also ...'(Yazaki, T. 1963). In India the traditional social differentiation in terms of caste was mirrored in as equally rigid pattern of residential differentiation, with the outcastes being segregated beyond the city limits. The patterns of residential differentiation and segregation in the modern city may be less obvious than is generally the case in the pre-industrial community, but the absences of walls and other physical signs of demarcation by no means implies any lessening of differentiation – let alone its disappearance.

SOCIAL DIFFERENTIATION IN THE CITIES

Residential differentiation and the resulting segregation of populations serve many purposes. Physical isolation symbolizes social isolation and decreases the chances of undesirable and potentially embarrassing contact. Furthermore, segregation may provide a means of group support in the face of a hostile environment and it may even lead to administrative efficiency. For whatever reason, residential differentiation characterizes both the pre-industrial and the industrial city, both the laissez-faire and the planned, both the Capitalist and the Socialist. The physical isolation of differing populations seems an inevitable concomitant of 'urbanism as a way of life'.

Sociological interest in the patterns of residential differentiation and segregation in the modern city has focused on those reflecting socio-economic status and ethnic variables. Although there are considerable problems at both the conceptual and operational levels in developing a valid measure of residential differentiation which can be used for comparative purposes. The existence of gross ethnic differences appears to be associated with relatively extreme residential differentiation. Residential dissimilarity correlates highly with social distance : the less desirable a given group is as intimate role-partners for another the greater will be their residential dissimilarity (Timms, 1969). Ethnic groups separated from each other by social differences are less likely to live in similar areas than are those who differ merely say in language. Thus, in the United States, Negroes exhibit consistently higher indices of residential dissimilarity when compared with the distribution of White Anglo-Saxon protestants than do members of various European migrant groups. Amongst ethnic minorities the degree of physical separation from members of the host society varies according to such factors as their similarity in terms of language, religion and occupation. The residential differentiation of socio-economic status groups within the city follows a similar pattern to that in terms of ethnicity. Again, the greater the social distance between two groups, the greater is likely to be their residential dissimilarity.

Like the society in which it exists, the modern city is highly differentiated. Different parts of the city are associated with different populations, with different opportunity structures, and with different reputations. The geographical framework of the city provides the basis for the emergence of a mozaic of social worlds. The increasing movement characteristic of modern society has almost certainly lessened the salience of location in the day-to-day lives of city-dwellers, but it remains the case that residence in one part of the city rather than in another has implication for a wide range of behaviours and biographies. The effects of location may be expected to be most pronounced on those whose daily movements are more or less confined to the bounds of their immediate neighbourhood – the young, the old, and the 'care—taker' – but the role of the local community in the critical socialization process and in the provision of a reference for social comparison purposes, ensures that the influence of the neighbourhood effect is felt across a variety of activities and groups. Different populations have different relationships to their locale and areas which are suitable for one group may be quite unsuitable for another. The diversity of urban life and society both reflect and demand a diversified community.

People living in one part of the city differ from those residents in other areas in innumerable ways. These differences are reflected in the variation in a great variety of demographic, socio-economic and cultural indexes across neighbourhood populations. In the modern western city, differentiation between neighbourhood populations is accountable for in terms no more than three or four underlying axes of differentiation: social rank, family status, ethnicity, and urbanism – mobility. The ecological structure of the city is formed by the inter-action of these properties as this is acted out in the locational decisions of the urban population and in the physical constructions of the city builders.

The differentiation of the urban community is the result of a complex interplay of forces. Residential differentiation involves both the overall structure of society and the decision – making activities of individual households. The attempt to understand the resulting urban structure must encompass aspects both of macro-sociology and social psychology.

At the individual level the choice of one residential location rather than another is a product of an involved sequence of aspirations, searches, and evaluations. In the hunt for a suitable address the preferences of the household for social rank, ethnic identity and way of life assume considerable prominence. Residential location may be seen as a mechanism for satisfying identity aspirations. Within the limits imposed by the information at their disposal and the economic resources which they possess, households attempt to attain their desired identities by locating amongst those who already possess the relevant statuses. At the cognitive level, it appears that information about the city may be organized in terms of those major social differentia which provide the bases for differential evaluation and reward and which provide the cross of self-identities. Different parts of the city are associated with different constellations of statuses and provide the foundation for different sets of identities, where a person lives is a symbol of the type of person he is. Aspirations for social rank may be satisfied by locating in neighbourhoods which have the reputation desired.

Aspirations for a given ethnic identity may be satisfied by residing amongst those whom one wants to be taken as being 'of one's own kind'. In either case, protection from undesirable contact and loss of desired statuses may be sought by removing oneself from the vicinity of the threatening group. Residential distance becomes a symbol of social distance and a means of preserving existing differentia. Different locations provide different facilities, preferences for different ways of life – differences which may be summarized in terms of such orientations as 'familism', 'carreerism', and 'urbanism' – involve an evaluation of the facilities which are offered by the available locations. Such characteristics as the size and the type of housing, the density of development, the age characteristics of the population and the accessibility of the site, assume considerable salience. Aspirations and outcomes rarely coincide in precise detail, but, as the result of feed back loops involving information flows and market processes, the aspirations of households and the supply of locations provide the parameters of a reasonably stable residential system whose structure reflects that of the encompassing society. Residential differentiation may be seen as a symbol of social differentiation.

The urban community does not exist in isolation. The city is both the creator and the creature of urban society. The limited differentiation characteristic of pre-modern society is reflected in the relative simplicity of the ecological structure characteristic of the pre-modern city. Both social and residential differentiation are based on a small number of closely – correlated criteria. Ascribed characteristics are uppermost and position in one status system is highly predictive to position in others. Different neighbourhoods are associated with populations which differ from each other in consistent ways across each of the status dimensions. Social rank is a prime determiner of way of life and provides the major axis of differentiation. With modernization and social mobilization the congruence between differentiating criteria breaks down. Traditional associations between statuses are upset. New bases of differentiation emerge and there is a growing structural independence between them. In the urban – industrial society universalistic, achievement–oriented criteria become major bases of status – allocation although the influence of such ascribed characteristics as ethnic origin may still remain important. Very generally, however, the process of modernization may be seen as eventuating in a shift from traditional forms of social differentiation and evaluation in which social rank, family characteristics, ethnic identity and migration experiences are all interrelated to systems in which each set of characteristics exercises its own independent effect. The ecological separation between social rank and family status indicants is believed to provide a sensitive measure of the degree of modernization to be found in the society concerned.

The spatial order of the city is founded on the desires and resources of its inhabitants as these are constrained and directed by the encompassing society. In the pre-modern city the simplicity of the social and ecological systems is reflected in that of the resulting spatial pattern. Self-contained quarters and a general zonal arrangement, with central-city location being the preserve of the elite, provide the basic plan. In the modern city a more complicated spatial order is apparent. Each differentiating property tends to follow its own distinct spatial pattern. They need to be within reasonable access to work and the attraction of the elite areas are reflected in the sectoral distribution of social rank. Once identified with a particular rank, developments in a given direction tend to perpetuate that identity. The attraction of new suburbs, with new houses and new standards of amenities, is reflected in zonal arrangement of family status. The younger the area, the more young people; the older the area, the more old people and the fewer families with young children. The zones in transition around the central business district and on the rural-urban periphery provide a haven for despised minorities and an attractive location for all those who welcome the anonymity and freedom from traditional social controls characteristic of the urban way of life. Since each set of differentiating properties is, to a greater or lesser extent, independent of all the others, the resulting spatial pattern is highly complex. It is unlikely that any simple model, stressing the influence of one or other spatial arrangement, will provide an acceptable description of the modern city.

Thus Human Society, is increasingly, an urban phenomenon. The city is becoming the principal setting for human behaviour. In the attempt to understand that behaviour or to plan for its control, it is essential that the characteristics of the urban setting are themselves understood. Neither the individual nor the community can be fully understood without knowledge of the other. The city not only shapes human behaviour but is, itself, the result of human behaviour. The urban mozaic is the matrix for urban society.

RESIDENCE AND SOCIAL STRUCTURE

Indian Studies

In India several subjective and quantitative analyses of the city structure have been made. Commenting on Indian city structure, Sjorberg stated that feudal cities in many ways are reverse to the industrialized modern cities. The high officials, big land owners, former Zamindars and upper caste people occupy the centre of the city. But as the time passed these traditional elites are being supplemented by new economic class, whose membership is based on education and position in government and non-government services. Sjoberg concludes: (a) pre-eminence of central area over the periphery, (b) certain finer spatial differences according to ethnic occupation and family type and (c) low evidence of functional differentiation in other land use pattern (Sjoberg, 1960).

Gist has made comparison of Indian and western cities. His study exhibited almost the same pattern as Sjoberg observed. According to Gist, people have tendency to choose their residences on the basis of racial and religious preferences which are symbol of wealth, power and social prestige. These bases are also seen in western countries. But in India caste preference and prejudice play an additional role in residential choice. One may discern "natural areas" that are occupied by particular caste. In almost all the Indian cities, particularly old cities, this pattern is observed. The religious nodes attract people around it. Religious monument of a particular religion is surrounded by people of that religion. Similarly, different pockets of the city formed by different caste can also be marked. Gist's study may be treated as a pioneer work on Indian city structure. Although he did not derive any dimension using variables, he put forward the idea which can be empirically tested (Gist, 1957).

Brush, through his study of Indian cities' ecology, has made notable contribution. Besides dealing with the above-mentioned characteristic of Indian cities, he tried to prove the traditional nature of Indian cities. The fringe of Indian cities is commonly occupied by low status people yet there are examples of peripheral sectors with new housing colonies where high economic class is grouped in a fashion similar to western cities. It shows the beginning of spatial restructuring of Indian cities. It is expected to continue, as urban income level increases. The facts brought in light by Brush are quite true, but he has presumably paid less attention to find them out in his empirical work (Brush, 1962).

In a detailed study on Calcutta, caste has been emphasized as major factor in the internal socio-economic differentiation. Caste and religion segregation are clearly visible here. The social space in Calcutta has been the scene of major confrontation between the enduring institution of old India – her caste, communities and diversity of ethnic heritages – and the pressures and values arising from the process of urbanization (Bose, 1965). Chatterjee has indicated that higher caste occupied the central locality for the lower caste the fringe in Howrah inspite of modern transport development ,while low income groups have been found to live near centre in Delhi. They are old residents as well as new migrants. The lower group seems to be surrounded by middle income group area and the upper income groups are shifting toward periphery in a sectoral fashion. The south Indian cities also revealed the same phenomenon. Rao and Ramchandran in their socio-economic survey of Vijayawada city observed higher caste, higher education and higher occupation occupying the city centre, and the periphery was characterized by reverse phenomenon (Rao, and Ramachandran, 1974). Caste system in India has not only influenced the pre-industrial cities, but it is visible even in the planned industrial city. For example, in Chittaranjan, quarters to employees were allotted on income basis for Punjabi and scheduled castes, are found segregated. Upper Hindu castes have resented the presence of scheduled caste in their locality. Even administration in Chittaranjan has not openly conceded that it favours the idea to allot quarters to scheduled caste at one or two places in towns to avoid the inter-caste unplesantries and conflicts.

The above studies made by Rao and Ramchandran used only aspects of population in their analysis. Even in population structure they have considered only occupation and education aspects. They did not include variables like age structure, level of education, housing conditions and amenities. None of the studies have marked any dimension and its spatial distribution in the city. Attempt to divide the city into homogeneous social or physical areas are lopsided. Such an attempt seems essential in drawing attention of government and planners for curbing unbalanced growth of the city. Further, economically as well as physically depressed areas, when recognized, may get special attention for its sound development by the government.

With the development of higher power electronic computers and advancement of powerful techniques it has become possible to use a large number of variables explaining different aspects of city structure. Several dimensions can be extracted and their scores mapped out. Combining the different dimensions homogeneous social areas may be delineated. In India, Manjoor Alam is the first geographer who successfully performed this job. His study on Hyderabad – Secunderabad twin city is based on his field observation. By analyzing fruitful data on education, occupation, income and housing characteristics, two dimensions emerged: (a) social rank based on literacy among general people, literacy among female for proportion of scheduled caste population and (b) urbanization based on workers in manufacturing, workers in commercial activities and workers in other services. He also tested the pattern of the dimensions. The social rank seemed to vary from centre to periphery in concentric manner and urbanization was highly segregated, and it showed little relationship to each other. He delineated the homogeneous area with the help of factor scores. Although it is a pioneer work in this direction, some more indigenous variables related to cultural aspects of the city might have given more refined results (Alam, 1965).

Some refinements over Alam's study have been made by a study made on Calcutta. In this study almost every aspect of city structure has been included. This study has successfully used Indian variables and produced ten dimensions. Some of them attested the western city dimensions but some new indigenous dimensions also emerged. For example, low incidence of functional differentiation in land use and increasing admixture of ecological pattern. It revealed family status as an independent dimension, but social-economic status for minority group membership is linked (Bose, 1968).

Urban Community

Writing on cities for social life, L. Wirth offered on organic formula for the definition of community. The term community, accordingly, refers to the symbiotic life of the people having a territorial or geographical base. It includes distribution in space of men, institutions and activities, and close living together on the bases of kinship and organic inter-dependence, and a shared life sustained by the mutual correspondence of interests (Reiss, 1964). In other words, the term refers to human life viewed from the stand point of symbiosis between different types of groups; and, it is different from society in which the characteristic mode of behaviour of the people is that of consensus. Although Wirth did not make it emphatically clear, it is self evident from the above broad definition of community that a city population does not in any way make a monolithic community. It means, therefore, that a large town or city consists of many communities or sub-communities such as natural areas or social areas. It may be added here that all the natural areas or social areas in a city cannot be called semi-urban pockets because some such areas may be either real slums of sub-human living conditions or posh colonies of the affluent.

While writing on the impact of urban environment on human temperament, Robert Park observed, "The process of segregation establish moral distance which make the city a mozaic of little worlds which touch but do not interpenetrate" (Park, 1952). The urbanites thus live in several different physically contiguous but otherwise widely separate cultural worlds. The continuous process of invasion, succession and segregation through which most of the people pass, as they come for settling in a city, leads to a great variety of settlements of people in social worlds. But it is a fact that different kinds of rationalities could be employed in meeting such exigencies. For instance, one may find that the census district classification is based on one kind of rationality, which may be different from that employed in arriving at natural social area or planned social area. For, the factor of size and density of population in the latter two types of areas may not coincide with a census tract or district which may be much smaller in size for varying in density. The term planned social area is used here just to match the natural social area concept, because planning for re-development of housing, etc. is now quite a common activity leading to rational organization of social units in which families with different prior background have to adjust to live. It is likely that all persons wished to live in a planned areas may not find it easy to adjust with others due to differences in education language, ethnicity, etc. of the people.

THE MULTI-ETHNIC SOCIAL WORLD OF SHILLONG

Shillong is a multi-ethnic city. It is a non-tribal town in a tribal setting. Only Mawkhar, Jaiaw, Mawlai and Malki, which are tribal areas having tribal population more than half of the total population of the area. The growth of the multi-ethnic groups has been because of the immigration from the surrounding rural areas as well as from the distant places including inter-state migration. These have greatly added to the growth of population in Shillong. It is said that Shillong is a place where people living here have varied ethnic background, just as they have in the Scottish highlands. There are dialects and dresses of diverse origin in this city.

Shillong is a cosmopolitan town and has migrants from almost every parts of the country. But only a few social groups are conspicuous by their population strength. They are the Assamese, Bengalis, Biharis (including those of eastern Uttar Pradesh), Khasis, Mizos, Nepalis, Rajasthanis and Punjabis. The distint ethnic groups by their concentration in a particular locality have acquired particular characteristic which become reflective through patterns of houses, types of construction, clustering of similar linguistic groups and alike neighbours, etc. The broad settlement patterns which can be classified are:

Assamese Settlements

Prior to the Indian independence, there were only a handful of Assamese residents in Shillong, having isolated settlements in Laban, Madan Laban, Kench's Trace, and Laitumkhrah. They came to Shillong in connection with government jobs. Even today they are hardly found engaged in any other activities. Most of these migrants can be identified in two phases, i.e. those who came before independence (mostly from upper Assam) and those who came afterwards (mainly from lower Assam). This can be ascribed to the good economic conditions and inquisitiveness to migrate to new areas for new jobs as well as better education being provided by the missionaries. Whereas in the post-independence period most of the migration can be reasoned as migration under political compulsion, mostly from erstwhile East Pakistan. The Assamese settlements in Shillong, today, are concentrated in Bishnupur, Kench's Trace, Motinagar (excluding Audit Estate Quarters), Forest colony. They are also settled in Laitumkhrah, Nongrim Hills, Fruits Garden and Lachumiere.

Bengali Settlements

The Bengalis came to Shillong with the shifting of the district headquarters from Cherrapunjee in 1864. In the beginning, they came as clerical staff to serve the government, and most of them were from Sylhet district of East Bengal. A large group of Bengalis also came from Hooghly district of West Bengal, who were mostly Muslims and were largely businessmen. In the early years of the growth of Shillong, the major portion of the commercial activities, including transport, was in their hands. While most of the Bengalis from Sylhet settled down in Jail Road and Police Bazar, and the Bengalis from Hooghly preferred Laban area. Since then these areas have continued to be the areas of attraction for new Bengali migrants to the city.

Rilbong, earlier a reserved forest under the cantonment authority, was acquired in 1928 by the Government and was distributed to its employees (mostly Bengalis) for residences. In Laitumkhrah proper the Bengali settlement started long before independence but in Bhagyakul and New Colony it has developed after independence. Umpling (formerly a forest land) was acquired by the Assam government for the settlement of East Bengal refugees. Their concentration began around 1960. The Bengalis are mostly to be found today in Laban, Lumparing cum Madan Laban, Rilbong, Lower Mawprem, Sunny Hills, Laitumkhrah and Umpling.

Bihari Settlements

The earliest migrants from Bihar to Shillogn were the foot soldiers and Sepoys, who walked on foot from Rajmahal Hills across Bengal plains in search of jobs in the aftermath of 1857s Sepoy Mutiny. Many of them got jobs as soldiers and policemen on the North Eastern Frontiers of the British Empire in 19th century. The Biharis followed the British administrators as personal attendants and servants, policemen, peons and sought employment in various services. They have been coming since the early years of the growth of Shillong. With the increased demand for various services their number has been ever increasing. They have monopolized in the lower category of jobs and services like barber, cobbler, butcher, washer man, mattress and quilt maker, and in bakery. They are a predominant group, dealing in milk and milk products, tea stalls, masonry works and betel leaves, etc. Some of them, however, have taken up new jobs like that of the provision stores, drivers, mechanics and clerks. Most of them are from the north-western districts of Bihar. About 45 percent of the Muslim population of Shillong are Biharis or belong to eastern Uttar Pradesh and most of them are in Jhalupara. The Biharis are concentrated in Bara Bazar, Garikhana, Palton Bazar, Laitumkhrah and Lalchand area.

Khasi Settlements

Though no record of the Khasis in Shillong is available for the early years, yet on the basis of the religious groups returned in the census as tribal or animist, some idea may be formed. In 1881 about 40 percent of the population of Shillong were the Khasis. Their relative share decreased though it has started increasing recently from 1941 till date.

Heavy concentrations of the Khasis in Shillong are in

Laitumkhrah, Malki, Mawkhar, South-east Mawkhar, Jaiaw, Mawlai and Nongthymmai. A small number of the Khasis (dealing in beef) are in Mawlai. Except for a few jobs of the barber, cobbler, sweeper, etc., the Khasis are present in every walk of life. Quite a good number of them are in office jobs. Some of the businesses like fish, vegetables, fruits and tea / tiffin supply to offices are mainly controlled by the Khasi women folk.

Mizo Settlements

Earlier the Mizos in Shillong were negligible about 0.34 percent of the total population in 1941 and it could rise 0.96 percent in 1961. Today they are considerable in number, constituting more than 3 percent of the total population of Shillong. The Mizos are concentrated in Madanriting, Happy Valley, Upper Nongthymmai, Nongrim Hills and Bishnupur (in the Meghalaya police battalion quarters). The Mizo settlements in Shillong are of recent origin. With the outbreak of large scale political disturbances in March 1966 and the strict government action thereafter, and re-grouping of villages in the Mizo Hills, a considerable number of Mizos, both poor and rich alike, left their home and settled in Shillong.

Nepali Settlements

The Nepali settlements in Shillong started after 1864 with the movement of the Sylhet Light Infantry. The creation of the 8th Gorkha Rifles brought more Nepalis to Shillong. The Nepali herdsmen towards the end of the last part of the 19th century were already present around Shillong. After the First World War when many of the retired army personnel were allotted land for settlement in Jhalupara, the Nepali settlement, increased significantly. Today they occupy a significant position and are present in every kinds of job- from domestic service, manual labour and grazing of cattle to white collar jobs. Many of them also work as porters, pony cart drivers, motor vehicle drivers casual labourers, milk and milk product sellers, etc. Though their settlements are scattered all over Shillong and its suburbs, yet they are predominantly in Jhalupara, Barapathar, Upper Mawprem, Palton Bazar and Nongmynsong (Lalchand Bustee). They are also present in Goalapatti, Garikhana, Lower Mawprem, Mawlai and Nongthymmai.

Settlement of Other Communities

The other groups include migrants from southern parts of the country mainly Kerela, Andhra Pradesh, Orissa, and elswhere, and they together account for only 6 percent of the total population. The Rajasthanis and the Punjabis are the two other important groups. The former have concentrated settlements in the commercial areas of Police Bazar, Gauhati-Shillong road and Bara Bazar, while the latter, most of whom are sweepers, belonging exclusively to Amritsar and Gurdaspur districts of Punjab, are concentrated at Goralane in Laitumkhrah and Sweepers lane near Bara Bazar. The people of other states are found scattered all over Shillong and are engaged mainly in Government Jobs.

Hence, on the basis of economic conditions of the inhabitants, age and quality of the buildings, availabilities of amenities and degree of congestion, the pattern of residential segregation takes a distinctive social form in Shillong, which is very similar to any other urban centre in the country.

D. INTERNAL STRUCTURE OF RESIDENTIAL AREAS

There are three well known classical models of city structure and growth, put forward by the American geographers and sociologists. The earliest of them is the concentric zone theory of Burgess, (Burgess, 1923). The essence of this model is that as a city grows, it expands radically from its centre to form a series of concentric zones-central business district, zone of transition, independent working man's homes, the zones of better residences and the commuter's zone. As the central business district advances, the transitional residential zone beings to deteriorate and the zone of better residences begins to move outwards. The quality and cost of the houses, therefore, increases with the distance from the centre and the residential density, consequently decreases. The Burgess model is based on a uniform case of transportation in all directions at every point.

The second model of the urban growth and spatial structure was formulated by Homer Hoyt (Hoyt, H. 1939) and is known as the sector theory. According to him the distribution of residential neighbourhood of various qualities neither have a random distribution nor form concentric circles, but are edge-sided, due to differences in land values, rents and the development of transport. Modern cities grow so large that they absorb many of their smaller neighbours and these control the pattern of landuse. The multiple nuclei model of Harris and Ullman (Harris and Ullman, 1945) is the modification of the previous two models. On the basis of economic conditions of the inhabitants, age of buildings, amenities and degree of congestion, it is possible to classify the residential areas of Shillong into four categories: high class, middle class, low class and slums. It is interesting to note that these residential areas in Shillong have followed some definite trends with the expansion of the town.

During the period of 1901 to 1991-2001 the city area of Shillong increased from 12.81 square km, with a population of 9621 in 1901 to 27.28 sq. km with a population 2,67881. Population growth was greater in proportion than the increase in the city area. So there was an increase in population density from 60 persons per hectare to 225 persons per hectare and the intra-city density varied from 2 persons per hectare to 63 persons per hectare. Thus, with the expansion of the city, most of the fringe areas became incorporated as intermediary zones while new fringes areas developed which served as the periphery.

In order to examine the internal structure of residential areas of Shillong, three population nuclei were recognised. From these concentric circles at an interval of half a kilometer were drawn and different types of residential areas were marked. This shows that high class residential areas have grown in eastern sectors of the first nucleus (Police Bazar-Mawkhar), in the western sector of the second (Laban), and in the northern, north-eastern and eastern sectors of the last (Malki) nucleus. The low class residential areas also have sectoral growth. The Police Bazar-Mawkhar nucleus is dominant. The internal structure of the residential areas of

Shillong shows a clear combination of the sector and multiple nuclei models.

The spatial structure of the city as a whole also can be examined with reference to the core, the intermediate zones and the periphery. The core consists of areas centred around the city CBD (in this case European Ward, Police Bazar and Bara Bazar). The peripheral zones consists of all the other census units of the agglomeration, outside the municipal boundary. The areas between the core and the periphery can be called, intermediate zones. Sharp differences exist between the core, intermediate and periphery areas of the city in terms of density, and residential housing and living conditions. (The oldest slum, sweeper colony, is situated in the C.B.D and is continuously growing in population numbers, both through natural and by migration). The density of the houses also decline in the same ratio from core to periphery. The other characteristic which show a similar declining pattern from core to periphery are percentage of workers in trade and commerce, the percentage of population in low income and middle income groups and percentage of rented houses. The city core thus acquires a special character by its centripetal pull and dominance, owing to the high concentration of workplaces, financial institutions, higher order shopping areas, transport terminals and lower order living conditions.

The classic study by Duncan and Duncan of Chicago city brings out the distribution in residential space of the different social and occupational categories in a strongly diversified manner and states that "the greater the social distance between the groups, greater the distance in their model of residential location" (Duncan, M, 1963). This tendency is again confirmed by the fact that groups with a strong index of spatial segregation are in the extreme groups both at the higher and lower levels in the scale of occupational stratification. Thus the more concentrated one is on the same space occupying the central zone of the urban area. The spatial stratification, therefore, brings out certain mechanisms in the organization of the city space:

(1) Social characteristics tend to form a spatial cluster. The closer these characteristics are the more they tend to group together in space.

(2) The essential principle that influences the distribution of housing in space is social prestige, the expression of which is social desirability (the preference of similar neighbours) and the negative expression of social distance (rejection by differentiated neighbours).

(3) The differential distribution of income, an expression of social sectioning (positive or negative) of a given kind of work determines accessibility to the residential space desired since it is subject to the laws of the market.

Thus, we can argue that variations in the income of residents, number of amenities and congestion of house create differences in residential areas. The economic conditions of the people have a bearing on the residential houses. Very often people of high income group stay in good residential areas. In Shillong, Lachumiere and Oakland are such areas inhabited by ministers, secretaries and other high officials as well as some high business class. The built up of the houses in these areas are good and spacious. Lumparing and Jhalupara, on the other hand, are inhabited by low income people. The residential areas in these localities are poor. The slums of Mawlai and sweeper lane of Bara Bazar are directly the result of the low income of their inhabitants.

The number of basic amenities such as water supply, electricity and good accessibility, etc. also vary greatly between one residential area and the other. The whole of Lumparing, large parts of Mawlai and some parts of Mawprem have only a few amenities and these are considered to be the low class residential areas. Motinagar, Laitumkhrah and Lachaumiere have good water supply, good educational institutions close to them and as such they are levelled as fair to good residential areas.

The degree of congestion or number of houses per unit

also indicates the category of the residential type, for example, Police Bazar, Mawkhar, Southeast Mawkhar and Malki are congested wards. Similarly parts of Jail Road, Mawprem, Jaiaw, parts of Laitumkhrah and the whole of Police Bazaar are residentially extremely congested. The houses in this area in general are poor in construction, old in age and small in size. In comparison to these, Laitumkhrah, Kench's Trace, European ward, parts of Jail Road and Shillong Cantonment with less than 20 houses per hectare are considered as spaciously built areas. Thus, the residential segregation can be easily identified on the basis of general conditions such as exterior look, building materials, age of the house, locational aspect, etc.

Within the city, therefore, distinct environments are created because of the different community, groups and classes which make up the urban society occupy distinct areas, having distinct occupations. All these account for a significant change in the pattern of residential segregation with the growth of the town. The residential area of the town covers 15.23 hectares, i.e. 48.47 percent of Shillong urban agglomeration. With a view to understand the ethnic mozaic of our universe, we did select two localities of Shillong: one a relatively mono-ethnic locality, Jaiaw – where Khasi the traditional inhabitants of the law predominate and two, an ethnically mixed locality of Laitumkhrah.

Laitumkhrah

Laitumkhrah is situated right in the middle of the Shillong city, occupying the largest area (i.e. 1.87 sq. km). The people living are of different cultures, i.e., ethnic groups and religions. It is composed of four wards (ward No. 1,2,3,and 4). The number of holdings in all the four wards is 1702 holdings (i.e. all groups). Till date there is no record of separate census data regarding separate ethnic groups. All groups are taken collectively. It is regarded as one of the biggest and most populous localities under Shillong municipalities. Its boundaries stretches as far as Abba restaurant on the west, touches Nongthymmai on the east, border with Pynthor on the north and Fish Dale on the south (Map 3.1).

Map 3.1

SHILLONG URBAN
SKETCH MAP OF LAITUMKHRAH

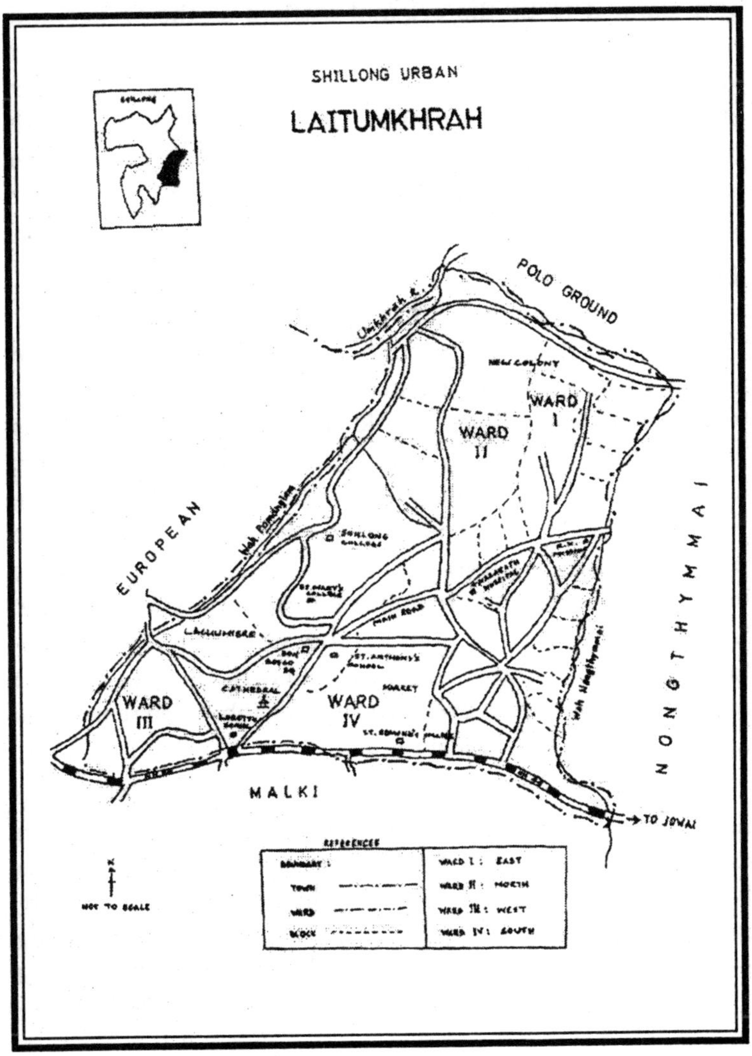

The locality is divided into various sub-localities such as (1) main and upland road (biggest in locality), (2) Nongkynrih, (3) Nongrim road, (4) Lum Sohra, (5) Nongrim Bah, (6) Nongrimmaw, (7) Demseiniong, (8) Lumawrie, (9) Bhagyagul, (10) New Colony. Laitumkhrah, being a municipal area, people of diverse ethnic background prefer to reside here. The Khasis, as reflected in Laitumkhrah locality, are said and claimed to be the original settlers or the 'indigenous people' of the land, Shillong. Possibly these four wards were identifiable in the distant past. However as the population of the town has grown up now, it is difficult to distinguish one ward from the other. Moreover, the basic social character and ethnic composition of Laitumkhrah remains the same that is a mixed ethnic locality.

Jaiaw

Jaiaw is situated in the northern part of Shillong city. The locality of Jaiaw is spread in three municipal wards (Ward No. 14,15,and 16). The number of holdings in all the three wards is (770) holdings. The locality is divide into various sub-localities such as (1) Jaiaw Pdeng, (2) Jaiaw Langsning, (3) Jaiaw Shyiap, (4) Jaiaw Lumpyllun, (5) Jaiaw Laitdom, (6) Jaiaw Lansonalane. By tradition it has been a pre-dominantly a Khasi inhabited residential locality. Its sub-localities, which were once upon a time distinguishable, but as the population grew in course of time, these sub-localities have merged with each other. But it goes without saying that it is almost exclusively Khasi inhabited residential areas in which others feel reluctant to reside (Map 3.2).

To understand "Ethnic Groups" and their relationship in Shillong, let us see what is the significance of such an existence and situation. The Khasis, are said and claimed to be the original settlers or the 'indigenous people' of the land, Shillong. They form the majority of the population in Shillong and have been able to play a dominant role in all aspects of life. Another unique point about the Khasis is that since

Map 3.2

SHILLONG URBAN

SKETCH MAP OF JAIAW

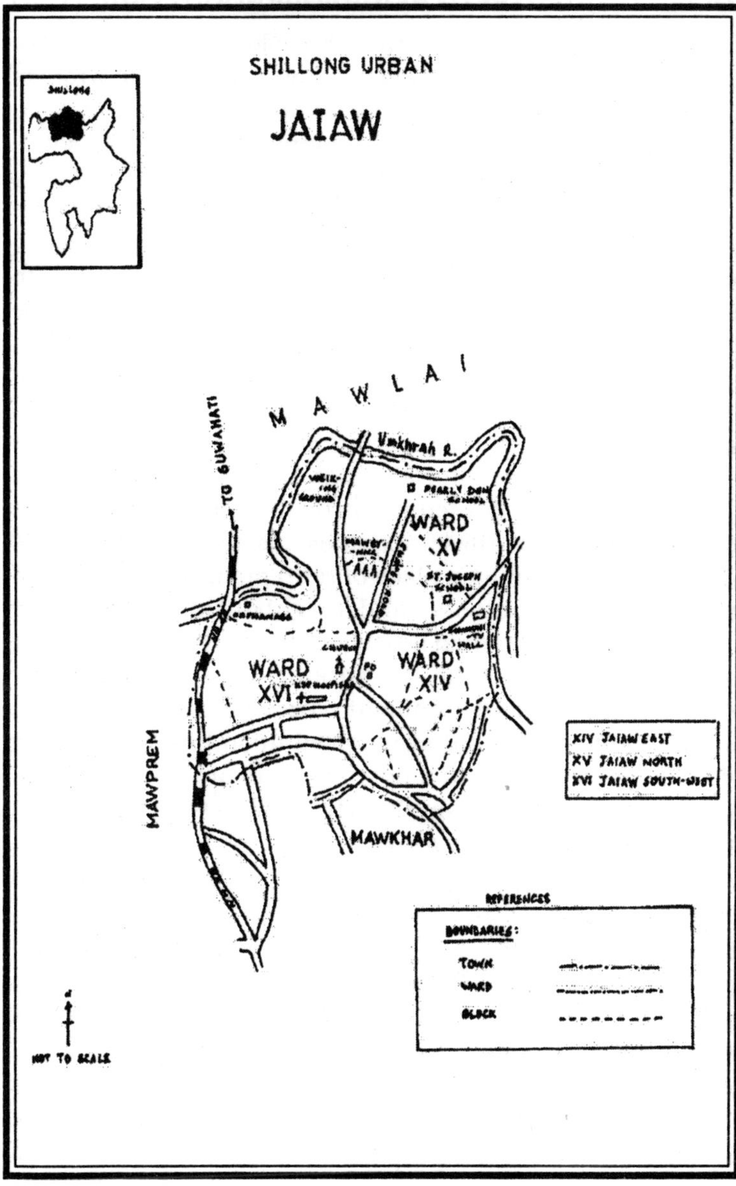

time immemorial and till today, they have been able to strictly follow the most ancient and most original matrilineal system.

SOCIAL ATTRIBUTES OF NEIGHBOURHOOD IN SHILLONG

Many years ago the American Sociologist E. A. Ross gave an interesting contrast between village and city. He wrote of the village that "when communication is difficult and slow, you accept as intimates your blood kinsmen and neighbours, because you see them often, you know them best and they are right at hand in case you need them. Even if they are dour and touchy, even if their ways and ideas grate upon you, you fraternise with them for there is no one else to consort with. Even though with them you cannot be quite yourself or follow your bent, you adapt yourself to them from dread of becoming a social outcast". In the Urban neighbourhood by contrast, "Modern methods of communication and transportation make possible a wise psycho-social and territorial range. The person's activities are not necessarily located in his home community, nor are the participants in these activities his neighbours. Home becomes significant as a place of retirement from the varied stimuli of social activity, and neighbouring tends to be redefined as unwarranted intrusion" (Ross, 1938), According to Reimer, "To relax from his working day, the city dweller seeks a residential environment where he will be free from the constant alertness that is forced upon him by mingling with the motley crowd of a heterogenous urban population. To relax in his private life, the city dweller wants to be with 'his own kind' " (Remer, 1952).

These comments on the neighbourshood may usefully be placed against Carpenter's definition so as to elucidate the principal functions of the neighbourhood. In his ideal type neighbourhood carpenter describes a "primary group sprit which is the fulcrum of neighbourhood life," but this is recognised as being broken down by all the processes of urbanization. Indeed, so much of an ideal type is carpenter's neighbourhood that it seems almost contradictory to think of it as an urban concept at all. Logically it could be argued that if all the forces of urbanism are "hostile" to the preservation of neighbourhood life, then how can the neighbourhood be an urban phenomenon? One is led to the conclusion that carpenter is speaking of a phenomenon that may have existed in the past when towns were small, communications were slow and when all the conditions of which Ross writes were present.

Both Ross and Reimer suggest that the neighbourhood is a place of retreat from the total urban life; it is a place where the individual can relax, with as little strain as possible, with people of his own sort. This means that he expects to find rest in the neighbourhood from the varied social contacts of city life, and their attendent social adjustments, in a social area where he can expect the people around him to think and act as he himself does. He thus has expectations of a similar outlook on life amongst his neigbhours, particularly in so far as life in the neigbourhood itself is concerned. So if people want to go out from his neighbourhood to work in other parts of the city, it they want to spend their leisure time in the city centre, these things do not particularly matter unless in some way they affect the neighbourhood.

Neighbourhood interaction is influenced by a number of factors. Recent studies, examining neighbourhood ties in urban surroundings, have indicated that neighbourliness is positively associated with length of stay in the city, length of stay in a particular locality and socio-economic status of the respondent. Individuals who have similar vocational, cultural, recreational or religious interest are likely to have more interaction if they reside close together in the same locality. Sweetser (1942) in his study of a neighbourhood in Bloomington, Indiana, found that the factors of sex and age were important. More pronounced than sex selection, however, was the tendency for people of all ages to associate preferentially with their own age group, both on the intimate and the acquaintance levels.

The respondants, we chose as the units of study as if they were atoms of urban units in Shillong and were required to respond on a number of issues like: their personal background, leisure hours, neighbourhood, social aggregation, and their involvements in the collective living. These responses have a distinct bearing on the inter-ethnic relations in the city of Shillong.

Social Background of the Respondents: Age, Marital Status, Religion and Ethnicity

It is evident from Table 3.1 that 15.81 percent of the Respondents were born before 1940. About 32.55 percent were born between 1941-50. While the majority of the respondents were born between 1951-60, and their percentage is 43.25. Only 8.37 percent of the respondents were born after 1960. It is also clear from the table that the age group of most of the respondents range between 50 to 60 years (which can be seen from Fig 3.1). Regarding the sex composition of the respondents, male constitute (125) 58.13 percent and female (90) 41.86 percent out of 215 respondents.

Table 3.1
Age group of the Respondents

YEAR OF BIRTH	FREQUENCY (215)	PERCENTAGE
Below 1940	34	15.81
1941-50	70	32.55
1951-60	93	43.25
1961 (+)	18	8.37
TOTAL	215	99.98

Source : Field Survey

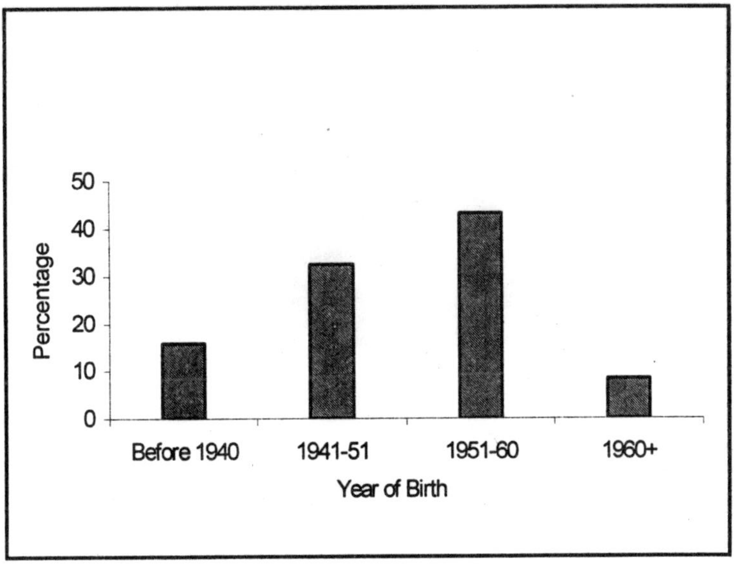

Fig 3.1 Age group of the Respondents

From Table 3.2 it is seen that out of 215 respondents, majority of them were married (80.93 percent). There were only 5.8 percent respondents, who were unmarried and similarly 7.90 percent and 4.18 percent respectively, were widowed and divorcees.

Table 3.2
Marital Status of the Respondents

RESPONSES	FREQUENCY (215)	PERCENTAGE
Unmarried	12	5.58
Married	174	80.93
Widowed	17	7.90
Separated	03	1.39
Divorced	09	4.18
TOTAL	215	99.98

Source : Field Survey

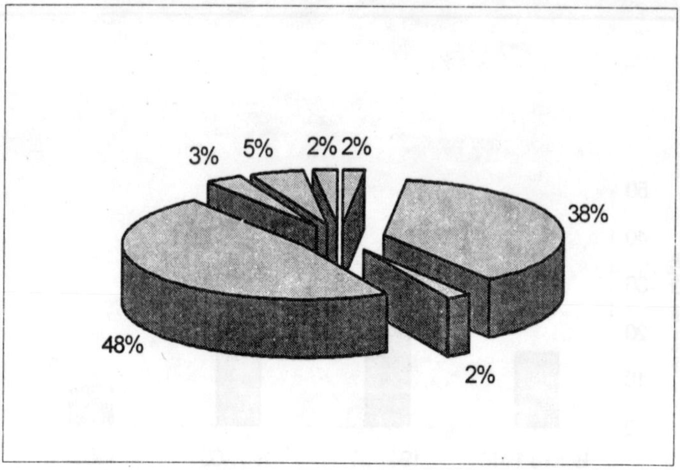

Fig-3.2: Religious Affiliation of the Respondents

Table 3.3
Religious affiliation of the Respondents

RESPONSES	FREQUENCY (215)	PERCENTAGE
Buddhist	04	1.86
Hindu	82	38.13
Seng Khasi	05	2.32
Christian	102	47.44
Sikh	07	3.25
Muslim	10	4.65
Any other	05	2.32
TOTAL	215	99.97

Source : Field Survey

Regarding the religious background of the respondents it can be seen from Table 3.3 that Christians dominated the scene with almost half of the respondents i. e (47.44 percent). These include Catholics, Presbyterians and other denominations as well. More than one-third of the respondents (38.13 percent) follow various forms of Hinduism. Religions like Muslims, Sikhs, Seng Khasi,

Buddhist and others constitute a small segment of the percentage from the total which can also be seen from (Fig 3.2.)

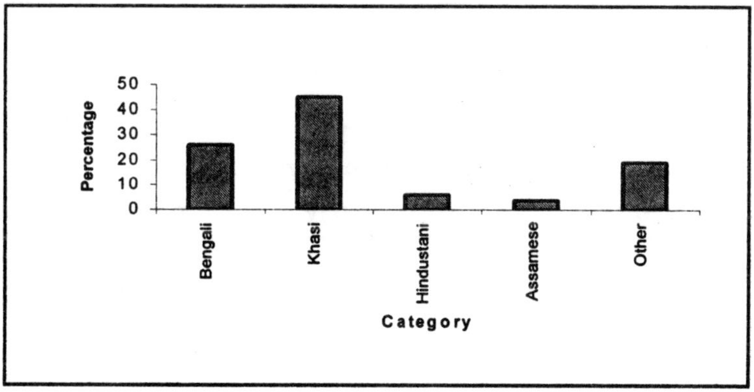

Fig-3.3: Ethnic Background of the Respondents

The ethnic background of the respondents is clear from Table 3.4. A considerable number of them were Khasis (45.11 percent). Next to them were the Bengalis, (26.04 percent). Hindustanis (6.04 percent) and the Assamese (3.72 percent) who were relatively less in number. Among the others, (19.06 percent) Nepalis, Oriyas, Punjabis, Tamils, Manipuris, etc. were counted. This can be seen from Fig 3.3 below.

Table 3.4
Ethnic Background of the Respondents

RESPONSES	FREQUENCY (215)	PERCENTAGE
Bengali	56	26.04
Khasi	97	45.11
Hindustani	13	6.04
Assamese	08	3.72
Others	41	19.06
TOTAL	215	99.97

Source : Field Survey

It is evident from Table 3.5 that 71.16 percent of the respondents were born in states other than Meghalaya. In response to the information about whether their place of birth was rural or urban, it is seen that majority of them were born in rural areas (53.02 percent) and the rest (46.97 percent) of them were born in urban areas.

Table 3.5
Place of Birth of the Respondents

RESPONSES	FREQUENCY (215)	PERCENTAGE
State (Meghalaya)	153	71.16
Other states	62	28.83
	215	99.99
Rural	114	53.02
Urban	101	46.97
TOTAL	215	99.99

Source : Field Survey

We enquired whether the respondents were permanent settlers of Shillong and found that as much as 85.11 pecent have been the permanent residents of Shillong.

The Table 3.6 shows that from among the non-permanent residents (32 out of 215) of Shillong (14.88 percent), 43.75 percent of them shifted to Shillong between 6 to 10 years back; 28.12 percent had shifted between 0 to 5 years back; which was followed by 21.87 percent who had shifted between 11 to 15 years back. And 6.25 percent (only two respondents) of them reported that they came to Shillong more than 16 years back. It is found out that most of the respondents migrated in search of jobs or business.

Table 3.6
The Years, when the Families of the Respondents Shifted to Shillong

YEARS	FREQUENCY (n = 32)	PERCENTAGE
0 – 5 years	9	28.12
6 – 10 years	14	43.75
11 – 15 years	7	21.87
16 – 20 years	2	6.25
21 (+)	00	00
TOTAL	32	99.99

Source : Field Survey

It was interesting to know the respondents who could speak, read and write languages other than their mother tongue. Thus it is evident from Table 3.7 that slightly more than half (40.46 percent) of the respondents could speak languages other than their mother tongue. It was followed by 29.30 percent of the respondents, who could speak, read and write. The respondents, who could not speak, read and write other than their mother tongue constituted 19.53 percent, and only 10.69 percent of the respondents could only read the languages other than their mother tongue.

Table 3.7
Proficiency of Languages Spoken by the Respondents

RESPONSES	FREQUENCY (215)	PERCENTAGE
Languages can speak, read and write	63	29.30
Languages can speak only	87	40.46
Languages can read only	23	10.69
Languages can write only	-	0
Languages can't speak & write	42	19.53
TOTAL	215	99.98

Source : Field Survey

Changing Authority in the families

We were interested in knowing the changing authority structure in the urban family. Thus we enquired of the respondents as to who enjoyed the greatest authority in the family during their father's generation. From the table (3.8) it is seen that 44.65 percent of the respondents informed that it was their mother who could enjoy the greatest authority in family affairs which was not surprising because the Khasis follow the matrilineal traditions in the family. More than (41.39 percent) of the respondents answered that it was their father who held the authority in the affairs of the family in the previous generation. In the case of the rest, it were either the grandfather (8.83 percent) or grandmother (5.11 percent). This information suggests that at least 15 percent of the respondents belonged to joint families.

Table 3.8
Changing Family Authority

RESPONSES	FREQUENCY (215)	PERCENTAGE
Father	89	41.39
Mother	96	44.65
Grand father	19	8.83
Grand mother	11	5.11
TOTAL	215	99.98

Source : Field Survey

Leisure Hours

With a view to understand the leisure time activities of the respondents we enquired as to how they spent their leisure time. From the table (3.9) it is evident that there is a vast difference in the outlook of Shillongites as compared to the cities / towns in the rest of the county. The social life seems to be alive as more than one-fourth (28.83 percent) of the respondents prefered visiting their friends. 17.20 percent have reported light readings, which was followed by 14.41 percent of them doing social and cultural works and (13.48 percent) by attending clubs. Games and sports accounted for 5.11 percent and among others which also constitute 20.93 percent included long driving, watching T. V., social visits etc. One may infer that the city remains largely informal as about 45 percent of the respondents reported to visiting friends, relatives and doing cultural works.

Table 3.9
Leisure Hour of the Respondents

LEISURE TIME	FREQUENCY (215)	PERCENTAGE
Attending Clubs	29	13.48
Visiting friends	62	28.83
Doing social/cultural work	31	14.41
Light reading	37	17.20
Games / Sports	11	5.11
Any other	45	20.93
TOTAL	215	99.96

Source : Field Survey

Aspirations

With a view to knowing aspirations of the respondents spending behaviour we enquired of them in case they had extra income, how would they spend it? Most of them would like to spend such amounts on the higher education of their children (20 percent). Another 19.06 percent would like to purchase Gold / Jewellery and other valuables. 17.20 percent of them reported that they would like to invest on shares / Fixed Deposits, Purchasing land, travelling and purchasing house were accounted for 13.95 percent, 12.55 percent and 10.23 percent respectively. 'Other' category included donation etc. were reported by only (15 respondents) which is 6.97 percent (Table 3.10).

Table 3.10

Future Aspirations of the Respondents

RESPONSES	FREQUENCY (215)	PERCENTAGE
Purchasing land	30	13.95
Purchasing house	22	10.23
Spending on higher education of children	43	20.00
Investing on shares/ Fixed Deposits and etc.	37	17.20
Purchasing gold/jewellery / other valuables	41	19.06
Travelling	27	12.55
Any other	15	6.97
TOTAL	215	99.96

Source : Field Survey

We felt desirable to understand how far our respondents were rooted to the town in terms of their owning urban property and pursuing various vocations available to them. For that we posed a number of questions pertaining to their attachments to the towns viz, their ownership of urban property, preference for settlement in the towns, preference for business / work, type of difficulties faced by them in doing their business and the facilities available in their respective localities for their various vocations. After administering the above questions we found that 67.76 percent of the respondents own a house in Shillong out of a total to 215, and the remaining 30.23 percent did not own a house in Shillong. 69.70 percent of the respondents preferred to own / rent a house in the locality, where members of their community live. About their settling down in Shillong if preference was given, majority of the respondents (69.70 percent) were willing to settle down in Shillong, whereas 30.23

percent did not want. Regarding the preference of having business or work in Shillong it is found that 81.39 percent are willing and 18.60 percent have answered in deformative manner.

View on problems and Amenities Available in the City

Urban citizens face many difficulties and the city of Shillong is no exception to this. While administering the questions as to whether they faced any difficulties in perusing their business / work in Shillong all the respondents replied in the affirmative. Some of the most common difficulties faced by them were getting permit / licences for business (44.18 percent), getting a rental house (25.58 percent). Another 23.72 percent admitted that they faced difficulties in purchasing a plot of land or house, which was followed by 6.51 percent, who said that they faced problems in getting admission to children in schools/colleges (as shown in Table 3.11 below). It can also be seen that there was no problems in getting new connections for water supply and electricity.

Table 3.11
Difficuluties Faced by the Respondents in the City of shillong

DIFFICULTIES	FREQUENCY (215)	PERCENTAGE
Getting rented house	55	25.58
In purchasing a plot of land or house	51	23.72
To get a new connection for water supply and electricity	00	00
Getting permit / licence for business	95	44.18
Getting admission to children in schools, colleges	14	6.51
Any other problems	00	00
TOTAL	215	98.99

Source : Field Survey

Table 3.12
Facilities Available in the Locality

FACILITIES	FREQUENCY (215)	PERCENTAGE
Good neighbourhood	89	41.39
Sufficient water facility	43	20.00
Pollution free zone	27	12.55
Safety and security	51	23.72
Near to market	05	2.32
TOTAL	215	99.98

Source : Field Survey

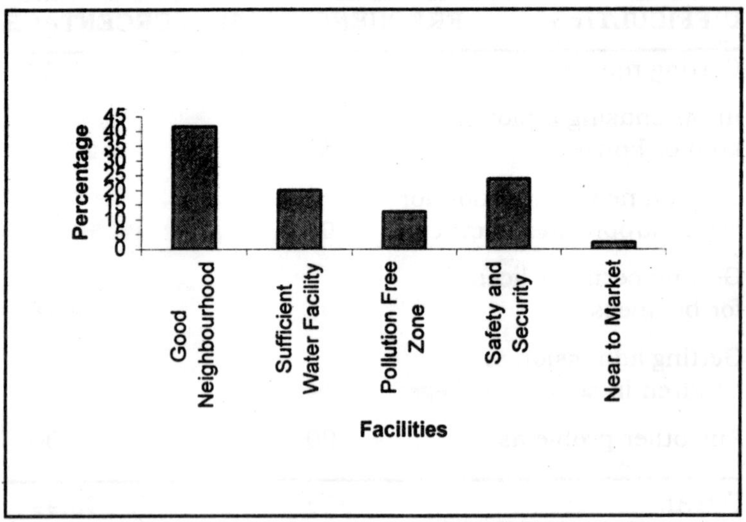

Fig-3.4: Facilities Available in the Locality

Every locality has a special importance where people reside. It was interesting to know what were the unique facilities available to the respondents in their locality, which were not found elsewhere. It is evident from the above table (3.12) that (41.39 percent) of the respondents reported that they had good neighbourhood. Safety and security (23.72 percent) and sufficient water facility (20 percent) were reported to be other categories of responses. 12.55 percent of the respondents informed of a pollution free zone, and only 2.32 percent indicated nearness to the market. Thus, it can also be seen from the above (Fig. 3.4), that in Shillong, good neighbourhood, safety, security etc. play a major role and people have their choice for selection of their residence.

We enquired of the respondents about their attachment to the locality, where they resided. All of them responded that the locality they reside were their choicest place to live in.

Social Circle

With a view to understanding the interaction of our respondents with people they most often met, 24.65 percent of the respondents met their intimate neighbour; 17.67 percent have reported that they met the member of their own community. Meeting the families with equal status and personal non-occupational friends accounted for 12.55 and 9.76 percent respectively. Meeting the economic 'notables' by the respondents were accounted for 8.37 percent. The other categories were religious people and high government officials, which were reported by 6.97 percent and 6.04 percent of the respondent respectively. Another 5.11 percent of them said that they met other people most often from the table mentioned below. Very small segment of the respondents (1.86 percent) met officers of the Armed Force and Police. Thus, from the table (3.13) one can infer that people in Shillong meet various groups of people in a closed circle.

Table 3.13

Most Frequently Met People By the Respondent

PEOPLE MEET	FREQUENCY (215)	PERCENTAGE
Members of your own community	38	17.67
Personal Non-occupational friends	21	9.76
High Govt. officials	13	6.04
Families with equal status	27	12.55
Political leaders	09	4.18
Officers of the armed force and police	04	1.86
Intimate neighbour	53	24.65
Religious leaders	15	6.97
Economic notables	18	8.37
Others	11	5.11
TOTAL	215	97.16

Source : Field Survey

Table 3.14

Persons Invited for Family Get-Together or / and cock Tail Parties

RESPONSES	FREQUENCY (215)	PERCENTAGE
Members of your own community	34	15.81
Personal Non-occupational friends	13	6.04
High Govt. officials	09	4.18
Families with equal status	27	12.55
Political leaders	03	1.39
Officers of the armed force and police	07	3.25
Intimate neighbour	67	31.16
Religious leaders	10	4.65
Economic notables	12	5.58
Others	33	15.34
TOTAL	215	99.95

Source : Field Survey

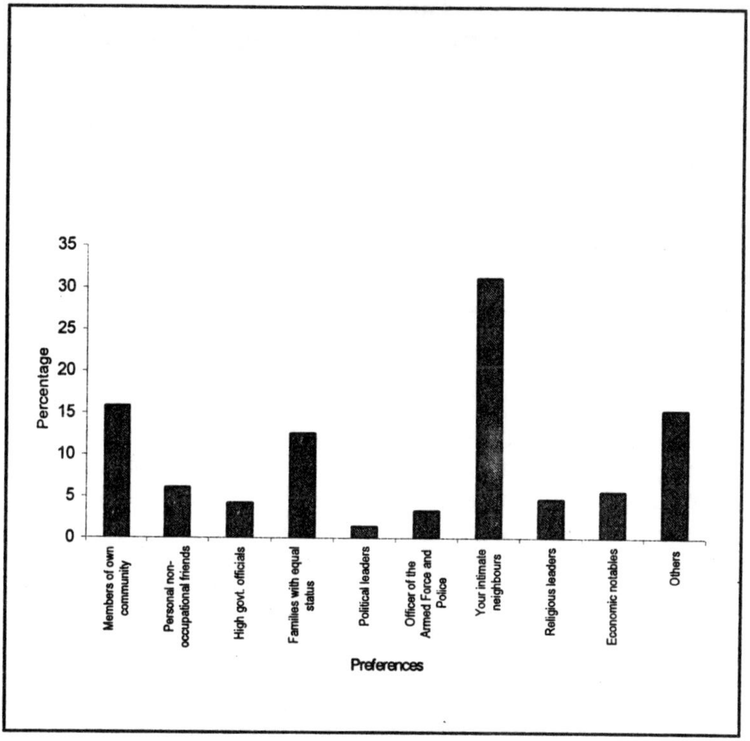

Fig-3.5: Persons Invited for Family Get-Together or / and cock Tail Parties

Similarly, it was interesting to know whom they informally invite for social get together or a cock-tail party. It is clear from the above table (3.14) and (Fig-3.5), that 31.16 percent of the respondents reported that they invited their intimate neighbours; 15.81 percent invited members of their own community; families with equal status and non personal occupational friends accounted for 12.55 percent and 6.04 percent respectively. The other categories of people, whom they called or invited, were less than 6 percent.

Thus, from the two tables (ie 3.13 and 3.14) one can see that similarity of the people whom they meet most often and whom they informally invite for social get together or a cock-tail party.

Table 3.15
Respondents Attitude towards Religions of Other Shillongites

RESPONSES	FREQUENCY (215)	PERCENTAGE
Respectful	145	67.44
Indifferent	47	21.86
Hostile	23	10.69
TOTAL	215	99.99

Source : Field Survey

With a view to understanding the views of the respondent on religions of other social groups in their neighbourhood, we enquired about their opinion. From the above table (3.15) it is evident that majority (67.44 percent) were respectful to other religions. In times of Christmas, or in times of Dussehras, Pujas or diwalis, or even during holies or 'id' other religious sects silently celebrate the occasion. But 21.86 percent admitted that they were indifferent, which was followed by 10.69 percent who were hostile to other religions in their neighbourhood. In fact, only Christians enjoyed their freedom and liberty, during festivals. Other religious groups do feel tensions and humiliations like the Muslims or the Hindus during their celebrations.

During religious festivities organised by different communities in the neigbourhood it may be noted that 50 percent of the respondents admitted that they were invited to participate.

It is interesting to know the pattern of work behaviour of the people, who prefered to take part in, if given a chance. From the table (3.16) below, it is evident that whatever they were doing at present, if offered to choose apart from their present occupation, this time (24.18 percent) of the respondents seemed to choose working in Non Governmental Organisations. Next comes social service (20 percent) which was followed by 15.81 percent in the religious rank. The respondents, who would like to join state politics accounted for 11.16 percent. The other categories like bureaucratic, army / police etc. were less than 10 percent. This shows that most of the Shillongites seemed to be enthusiastic about adding their contribution to the Non Governmental Organisations, social service, religious rank, so as to ensure a voluntarly services to mankind rather than serving the Government or a particular individual. The public seem to be enlightened-on public affairs. Which can also be seen from (Fig. 3.6) below.

Table 3.16
Preferred Institutions in which Respondents propsed to participation

RESPONSES	FREQUENCY (215)	PERCENTAGE
Join state politics	24	11.16
Join the religious bank	34	15.81
Join bureaucrary	19	8.83
Join N. G. O.	52	24.18
Become a top business man	26	12.09
Join army/Police	13	6.04
Join social service	43	20.00
Join armed rebellion	00	00
Others	04	1.86
TOTAL	215	99.07

Source : Field Survey

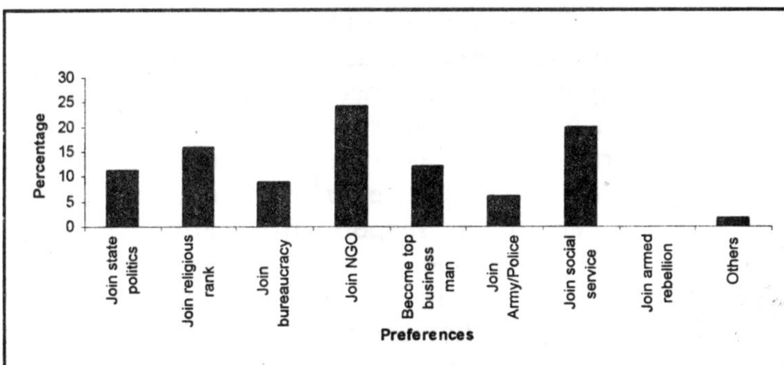

Fig-3.6: Preferred Institutions in which Respondents proposed to participation

Table 3.17
Showing Involvment of the Respondents in Cultural Social Associations

RESPONSES	FREQUENCY (215)	PERCENTAGE
Indifferent	29	13.48
Any ordinary member	73	33.95
Activity engaged in activities	56	26.04
Very active as an office bearer	31	14.41
Hostile	26	12.09
TOTAL	215	99.97

Source : Field Survey

It can be seen from the above table (3.17) that 33.95 percent acted as ordinary members to the social/cultural associations. Those who were actively engaged in such activities accounted for 26.04 percent, which was followed by 14.41 percent of those who were very active as office bearers. 13.48 percent and 12.09 percent of the respondents respectively admitted that they were either indifferent to cultural activity or hostile against cultural / social association of their community. Thus, one learns that as much as three fourths of the respondents were active in cultural affairs of their community.

With a understanding the relationship of the different ethnic groups in Shillong we enquired of the respondents to identify their closed circle of friends. From the Jaiaw locality, where the population is homogeneous, it was found that all the respondents mentioned their own community people as their intimate friends. Whereas in the locality of Laitumkhrah the responses received was quite different. In Laitumkhrah around 20 percent of the respondents mentioned their intimate friends, those who did not belong to their own community. For example, in Laitumkhrah Bengali respondents reported that their intimate friends were Assamese, Marwari, Nepali.

We were also interested to know about the urban neighourhood of Shillong city. Thus we have enquired from our respondents to mention atleast 3 names of the families from their neighbourhood with whom they had most intimate relations. From the Jaiaw area, it has been found that all the respondents said it is their own people in their neighbourhood with whom they have intimate relations. This is an obvious reason, as in that locality no other ethnic groups are settled. Whereas in Laitumkhrah area, the answer received from the respondents were quite different. Here the respondents intimate relation in the neighbourhood was of mixed group. For instance a Punjabi respondent said that his most intimate neighbours are the Bengalis, Hindustanis, whereas a Bengali's intimate neighbours were Kerelian, Manipuri etc.

From the above we drew two lessons; one, that even in the most cosmopolitan city like Shillong there are ethnically exclusive localities as they may be found in the traditional rural Khasi tribal settings. Secondly, the responses from the other locality indicate the symptoms of mixed social experience found in the urban centres elsewhere.

Shillong is the most cosmopolitan town in the North-east India and it has immigrants from almost all the states of the country. But only some social groups are conspicuous by their strength. They are Assamese, Bengalis, Khasis, Nepalis, Punjabis, Hindustanis and Marwaris. The distinct ethnic groups by their concentration in a particular locality acquired particular characteristics, which became reflective through patterns of houses, types of construction, clustering of similar linguistic groups and alike neighbours etc. The economic condition of the inhabitants, availabilities of amenities and degree of congestion, the pattern of residential segregations takes a distinctive from in Shillong, which may be similar to any other urban centre in the country.

According to 1961 census there were as many as 187 languages in the country. Out of which, 94 languages were spoken by less than 10,000 persons each, and 23 languages together account for 97 percent of the total population of the country. The picture becomes more confusing in 1971, when the census report declared as many as 3,000 languages spoken by different communities (Ahmed, Ali. 1983).

From the census figure of 1981, it is clear that after the independence of India, the establishment of office complexes in Shillong got momentum and the various ethnic groups flocked to it. Furthermore, with the partition of India in 1947 and consequent influx of refugees from East Pakistan in 1964 and from Bangladesh in 1971 greatly accentuated the population growth in Shillong. Many other ethnic groups from other states of this country also moved into this town for business, contract works and other vocations. Some Nepalis settled in the town as soldiers, coolies, handy-boys, office workers, and in various other petty jobs. These ethnic groups co-existed in Shillong and their inter-ethnic relation was marked by cordiality in the beginning. However, though inter-ethnic relations was cordial and inter-dependent for economic existence, under current strained relations emerged in course of time, which became evident from occasional street clashses and conflicts. This came to the forefront, when an open communal conflict broke out in 1987 with the Nepalis and in 1992 with the Hindustanis, resulting in huge loss of property and causing human misery. A type of ethnic intimidation continues to be prevalent, which may be seen in the threats and intimidations often used as method of election campaining. However, responsible citizens are aware of the fact that they have to live together and as such inter-ethnic marriages also take place and efforts are quickly made to restore normalcy in social harmony.

The population in Shillong can be classified into two groups, (a) Tribal and (b) Non-tribal. The major tribal population in Shillong consists of the Khasis, inclusive of the Jaintias. Among the non-tribal population, Bengalis, Biharis, Nepalis, Assamese, Punjabis, Marwaris may be enumerated.

In case we consider 10 percent and above population of this town as speakers of a major language, one finds four major ethnic groups in Shillong; Khasi, Bengali, Nepali and Hindustani (speakers of Hindi and Urdu together). Khasi is spoken by almost half of the urbanites in Shillong. Similarly,

Bengali is spoken by about 20 percent of the population, Nepali by about 12 percent of the Shillongites, and Hindustanis another by 10 percent urban residents. Incidentally, ethnic groups have been major social players in the life of Shillong. The Assamia is spoken by 6,367 persons. There were two other languages spoken by about 1 percent residents of Shillong, which may be termed as the minor languages spoken in Shillong. These are the Punjabis (2,647) and the Garos (2,012). However, there were many other minor languages such as Bodo, Manipuri, Kuki, Mizo, Naga, Sema, Tibetan, Lotha, Dogri and Tangsa. English may be enumerated, whose speakers are small in number. Linguistic variety adds to the heterogeneous character of the town.

Thus, the population composition of Shillong city is ethnically dominated by the Khasi, Bengali, Nepali, Hindustani, Assamese, Punjabis and Marwaris. Linguistic uniformity brought greater harmony amongst the different ethnic groups, who used to differ not only in their spoken languages, but also in their administrative organisations, customary laws, and social and societal institutions. Such harmony as is expected, has been at work positively, in the growth of Shillong despite the fact that different groups maintain their identities.

Inter-ethnic relationship within the city generally appears to be harmonious not only in the economic field, but also in a social context. Various ethnic groups are almost equally important as a business community and apparently there is nothing to indicate sectorisation or polarization of communities in matters of business dealings. Any such apprehension is further thwarted by the fact that social interaction between different ethnic groups with regard especially to marriage is very common. As a matter of fact, at a superficial level there is no distinction among the urban ethnic groups. In the next chapter, we propose to uncover the extent of modernity among the citizens of Shillong

4

THE CONTEXT OF MODERNITY

MODERNITY

The concept of modernity has emerged as one of the central themes in social analysis. It seems destined to assume an even more prominent place in the thinking of behavioural scientists. The term may refer to two quite different objects. As used to describe a society, "modern" generally means a national state characterized by a complex of traits including urbanization, high levels of education, industrialization, extensive mechanization, high rates of social mobility and the like. When applied to individuals, it refers to a set of attitudes, values, and ways of feeling and acting, presumably of the sort either generated by or required for effective participation in a modern society. Culturally, modernity is portrayed as a consistent set of values and general orientations permeating a society. Its content is perhaps best described in terms of the parsonsian pattern variables: a culture that is universalistic rather than particularistic, defines roles in specific rather than diffuse terms, and allocates rewards on the basis of achievement and not ascription.

The psycho-social definition of modernity is of greater theoretical importance. First, it possesses an autonomous meaning content; second, the interest it arouses is not limited to validation of its hypothesized existence but extends to its strategic role vis-à-vis broader processes of societal development. The relationship of modernity thus defined to general economic development is not entirely clear. For some, most of the traits associated with modernity are consequences of life in industrial settings. Such was the dominant trend of early urban sociology as it sought to specify consequences of urbanism on human personalities. Simmel in particular made a compelling case for rationality – the dominant characteristic of modern man – as a functional adaptation to the overwhelming stimulation and complexities of metropolitan life (Simmel, 1950).

In contrast, contemporary writers have envisioned psychological modernity as a determinant of social and economic development. If not sufficient, modernity is defined as at least a necessary condition for these societal goals. Arguments of this nature are based, implicitly or explicitly, on a logic similar to Max Weber's theory of the Protestant ethnic: a unique set of psychological orientations which, if present in sufficient numbers, will motivate major changes in the economic structure of a society (Weber, M. 1904). Unfortunately, none of the recent theories possesses the attention to historical detail and systematic description of intervening mechanisms characterizing Weber's argument. Instead, a psychological independent variable is posted, on grounds of general historical plausibility, as determinant of societal development.

The role of modernity as cause of industrialization and development is, of course, far more strategic to Third World Nations. However, prior to examining whether modernity is in fact cause or merely consequence of accelerated economic development, it is necessary to establish beyond doubt its empirical existence as a unique psycho-social dimension. While cross-national studies such as those conducted by Daniel Lerner (1964) and Alex Inkeles (1969) report a basic syndrome identifiable with modernity, other empirical research has yielded mixed or negative results. In addition, cogent critical analyses by Gusfield and Bendix (1967) cast doubt on a prior assumptions that mixtures of traditional and modern traits are necessarily transitional and short-lived.

Modernity is generally viewed as an asset, the more an underdeveloped nation has of it, the better. Underlying this value orientation is the assumption that a greater number of modern men will promote "dynamic enterpreneurship" and hence, accelerated economic growth. It is often forgotten that much of what goes into forming a modernity syndrome in the developed West is the consequence of historical processes of urbanization and industrialization. Defining modernity as a positive force in the socio-economic growth of developing countries may account to an uncritical extrapolation of consequences into causes. There is a historical naivete in believing that if the psycho-social product of centuries of social and economic evolution can just be reproduced in an underdeveloped context, it will bring – by association – the structural arrangements that gave rise to it in the first place.

Modernity in the West is not identical with underdeveloped modernity if for no other reason than that the first is, in the broadest sense, the organic product of internal processes of structural differentiation and growth while the second is, to a large extent, the product of cultural diffusion. The exposure which urban residence, years of education, and the vantage point of higher socio-economic status afford the individual is, for the most part, exposure to influences emanating from the West.

Modernity may thus owe its cross national stability to being largely an "import product" from the same source and, hence, artificially superimposed on the social structures of receiving countries. Saying that its presence in the latter is an unmixed blessing amounts to a subtle form of ethnocentrism. To the contrary, it is possible to argue that massive modern orientations in an underdeveloped context may be indifferent or, in fact, positively detrimental to accelerated economic growth.

Modernity is not a sacrifice – legitimating ideology. High aspirations and individualism make modernity non-ascetic: Secularism and rationality make it non-ideological. Prized as utilitarian rationality may be in developed contexts, it has often been irrational embracement of ideology, which has provided the force behind initial economic growth.

Premature modernity-in-underdevelopment, excessive aspirations and secularism, and sophistication bearing no relationship to its social and economic context may make of the most westernized sectors the main obstacle to initial stages of national development. As Horowitz states: "Interestingly, where modernism has been extremely applied, industrialization has had little success. Far from serving as a demonstration effect of the advantages of industrialization, modernism serves to reinforce the existing social structure by showing how it is possible for a small section of the population to share in the goods of the scientific technological world without altering the forms of human relations or the character of social production. Thus, modernism may serve, ironically, to underwrite traditionalism and not to displace it" (Horowitz, 1966).

THE MODERNIZATION OF MAN

The characteristic mark of the modern man has two parts; one internal, the other external; one dealing with his environment, the other with his attitudes, values and feelings.

The change in the external condition of modern man may be summarized by reference to a series of key terms: urbanization, education, mass communication, industrialization, politicization. These terms signify that in contrast to his forebears living in the traditional order of his society, the modern man is less likely to work on the land as a farmer and is more likely to be employed in a large and complex productive enterprise based on the instensive use of power and advanced technologies. The various economies yielded by the concentration of industry in certain sites and the further demands of those industrial concentrations make it likely that the contemporary man will live in a city or some other form of urban conglomeration. Here, he will experience not only crowding but access to all manner of resources and stimulation characteristic of urban life. Inevitably, one of these stimuli will be the media of mass communication: newspapers, radio, movies and perhaps even television. His experience of new places and ideas will be augmented by the impact of schooling, if not directly for him, than for his children, who may carry the influence of the school into the home. He is much more likely to have some connection with politics, especially on the national scale, as he is more exposed to mass communication; more mobilized in the surge of urban life, more courted by the competing political movements that seek his support as he may enlist their aid to replace that of the chief, the patron, the family head whose assistance he would ordinarily have sought in his native village. Indeed, another mark of the contemporary man is that he will no longer live enmeshed in a network of primary kin ties, perhaps supplemented by ties to a small number of fellow villagers, but rather will be drawn into a much more impersonal and bureaucratic milieu in which he is dependent for services and aid in times of distress on persons and agencies with which he has a much more formal and perhaps tenuous relationship.

These are all attributes of his life space that may impinge on the modern man, but in themselves they do not constitute modernity. The densest urban centres may still shelter the most traditional network of human relations; the media of mass communication may mainly disseminate folk ideas and traditional wisdom factories may run on principles not far different from those of the estate and politics may be conducted like an extension of the village council. Although his exposure to the modern setting may certainly contribute to the transformation of traditional man, and although that setting may in turn require new ways of him, it is only when man has undergone a change in spirit – has acquired certain new ways of thinking, feeling and acting – that we come to consider him truly modern.

Although there is no single standard definition of the modern man that all accept and use, there is quite good agreement among students of the modernization process as to the characteristic that distinguish the more modern man from the more traditional.

The first element in the definition of the modern man is his readiness for new experience and his openness to innovation and change. We consider the traditional man to be less disposed to accept new ideas, new ways of feeling and acting. Thus, in our sense, a man may be more modern in spirit, even though he works with a wooden plow, than someone in another part of the world who already drives a tractor. The readiness for new experience and ways of doing things, furthermore, may express itself in a variety of forms and contexts: in the willingness to adopt a new drug or sanitation method, to accept a new seed or try a different fertilizer, to ride on a new means of transportation or turn to a new source of news, to approve a new form of wedding or new type of schooling for young people. Individuals and groups may, of course, show more readiness for the new in one area of life than another, but we can also conceive of the readiness to accept innovation as a more pervasive, general characteristic that makes itself felt across a wide variety of human situations. And we consider those who have this readiness to be more modern.

The second element of the modern man is that, we define a man as more modern if he has a disposition to form or hold opinions over a large number of the problems and issues that arise not only in his immediate environment but also outside of it. Some pioneering work on this dimension has been done by Daniel Lerner (1964), who found that the individuals within any country, and the populations of different countries, in the middle - East varied greatly in their ability or readiness to imagine themselves in the position of prime minister or comparable government leader and thus to offer advice as to what should be done to resolve the problems facing the country. The more educated the individuals and the more advanced the country, the greater was the readiness to offer to opinions in response to this challenge. The more traditional man, we believe, takes an interest in fewer things, mainly those that touch him immediately and intimately; and even when he holds opinions on more distant matters, he is more circumspect in expressing them.

We mean by this that he shows more awareness of the diversity of attitude and opinion around him, rather than closing himself off in the belief that everyone thinks alike and, indeed, just like him. The modern man is able to acknowledge differences of opinion without needing rigidly to deny differences out of fear that these will upset his own view of the world. He is also less likely to approach opinion in a strictly autocratic or hierarchical way. He does not automatically accept the ideas of those above him in the power hierarchy and reject the opinions of those whose status is markedly lower than his.

A third theme we deal with at some length is that of time. We view a man as more modern if he is oriented to the present or the future, rather than to the past. We consider him as more modern if he accepts fixed hours, that is to say, schedules of time, as something sensible and appropriate, or possibly even desirable, as against the who thinks these fixed rules are something either bad or perhaps a necessity, but unfortunately also a pity. We also define a man as more modern if he is punctual, regular and orderly in organising his affairs. These things can be very complicated, and this is a good opportunity to pint out that it is a mistake to assume that our measures of modernity differentiate between traditional and non-traditional people as they would ordinarily be defined. For example, the Maya Indians had a better sense of time than their Spanish conquerors, and they preserve it to this day. The qualities we define as modern can, in fact, be manifested in a people who seem to be relatively 'unmodern' when you consider the level of technology or the amount of power they have. We are talking about properties of the person, which in turn may be a reflection of the properties of a culture that could emerge in any time or place.

A fourth theme that we include into the definition is planning. The more modern man is oriented toward and involved in planning and organizing and believes in it as a way of handling life. A fifth and important, theme we call efficiency. The modern man is the one who believes that man can learn, in substantial degree, to dominate his environment in order to advance his own purposes and goals, rather than being dominated entirely by that environment. For example, a man who believes in efficacy is more likely to respond positively to the questions, "Do you believe that some day men may be able to develop ways of controlling floods or preventing destructive storms?" The more efficacious man, even though in fact he has never seen a dam, would say, "Yes, I think that some day man could do that".

Sixth, an element we consider part of the modern complex and include in our set of themes is calculability. By our definition, the modern man is one who has more confidence that his world is calculable, that other people and institutions around him can be relied on to fulfil or meet their obligations and responsibilities. He does not agree that everything is determined either by fate or by the whims of particular qualities and characters of men. In other words, he believes in a reasonably lawful world under human control.

The seventh theme that we stress is dignity. The more modern man, we feel, is one who has more awareness of the dignity of others and more disposition to show respect for them. We feel this comes through very clearly in attitudes toward women and children.

The modern man has more faith in science and technology, even if in a fairly primitive way. This provides our eight theme. Ninth, we hold that modern man is a great believer in what we call, for this purpose, distributive justice. This is to say, he believes that rewards should be according to contribution, and not according to either whim or special properties of the person not related to his contribution.

Just as modernity seems to be defined not by any one characteristic, but by a complex of traits, so we find that no one social force, but rather a whole complex of influences, contributes to the transformation from traditional to modern man. Within this complex of forces, however, one certainly assumes pre-eminence: namely, education. Almost all serious scientific investigations of the question have shown the individual's degree to modernity to rise with increases in the amount of education he has received. We may still say that education, especially in schools emphasizing the more modern type of curriculum, seems to be the most powerful factor in developing a population more modern in its attitudes and values. This effect depends in part on the direct instruction provided, but we assume as well that the school as a social organization serves as a model or rationality, of the importance of technical competence, of the rule of objective standards of performance, and of the principle of distributive justice reflected in the grading system. All these models can contribute to shaping young people in the image of the modern man.

There is little agreement as to the rank, order of influences, other than education, that we see affecting the degree of modernization of individuals. Many analysis of the problem propose the urban environment as the next most important input. The city is itself a powerful new experience. It encourages, and indeed to some degree obliges, the individual to adopt many new ways of life. By exposing men to a variety of ways of living, a wide range of opinions and ideas, increased mobility, more complex resources of all kinds, it accelerates the process of change. At the same time, in the city the prospect is greater that the individual will be relatively free from the obligations and constraints placed on him in the village by his extended kinship ties, the village elders, and the tight community of his neighbours. These structural differences free the individual to change; but, of course they do not in themselves guarantee that he will change in ways that make him more modern. In many cities, there are powerful examples of rationality, of the use of technology to master the physical demands of life, or rewards adjusted to technical skill and competence, of the value of education, and of the guarantee of human dignity under law. But many great cities also provide powerful lessons that run counter to these modernizing influences on every score. If they breed a new type of man, they hardly make him in the image we have called modern. In addition, under conditions of very rapid growth, the city is often unable to absorb and integrate all the immigrants, so that on the outer edges or in the older districts of the city, huge slum communities may develop in which people are in the city but not of it, cut off from many of its benefits and from the modernizing influence of urban life.

One source of modernization, which generally accompanies urbanization but it also an independent influence, is mass communication. Almost all studies of the growth of individual modernization show that those who are more exposed to the media of mass communication have more modern attitudes. Since such exposure, especially in the case of the newspaper, depends on literacy and education, it is important to stress that the modernization effects of the mass media can be shown to exert their influence within groups at almost any educational level. Of course, there remains the possibility that it is the man with modern attitudes who seeks out the mass media, rather than that the media make the man modern, but there seems little reason to doubt that the influence is at least mutual. These media greatly enlarge the range of human experience with which the individual can have contact, even if only vicarious. They constantly present and illustrate new tools, items of consumption, means of transportation, and a myriad of new ways of doing things. They show examples of efficacious behaviour of the most powerful kind in the building of dams, the taming of floods, the irrigation of deserts, and even the conquest of space. They also provide models of new values and standards of behaviour, some of which are far beyond the reach of most men, but many of which can be copied and do influence behaviour directly. As in the case of urban influences, we must acknowledge that the media of communication can and often do carry messages that mainly reaffirm traditional values, beliefs and ways of acting or disseminate to concept of the new that is nevertheless not congruent with the model of the modern man here described.

Another source of modernizing influence is the development of the national, state and its associated apparatus of government bureaucracy, political parties and campaigns, military and para-military units, and the like. The more mobilized the society, the more dedicated the government to economic development and spreading the ideology of progress, the more rapidly and widely may we expect the attitudes and values of modernity to expand. Some of the agencies of the state – in particular, the army – may play an especially important role in introducing men to the modern world, both in the direct instruction they offer and indirectly in the model of routine, scheduling, technical skill, and efficacy that inheres in many of their operations. Here again, however, we must acknowledge that the power of the state may also be used to reinforce more traditional values: politics may be conducted in a way that hardly sets an example of modern behaviour, and armies may be run so as scarcely to induce a man to exert himself, to practice initiative, or to respect the dignity of others.

Thus Modernity may refer to two quite different objects. Firstly, "Modern" generally means a nation-state characterised by a complex of traits including urbanization, high levels of education, industrializations, extensive mechanisation, high rates of social mobility and the like. Secondly, when applied to individuals, it refers to a set of attitudes, values, and ways of feeling and acting, presumable of the sort either generated by or required for effective participation in a modern society. Culturally, modernity is portrayed as a consistent set of values and general orientations permeating a society. Its content is perhaps best described in terms of the Parsonsian pattern variables: a culture that is universalistic rather than particularistic, it defines roles in specific rather than diffuse terms, and allocates rewards on the basis of achievement and not ascription. The psycho-social definition of modernity is of greater theoretical importance. Most of the traits associated with modernity are consequences of life in industrial settings. Such was the dominant trend of early urban sociology as it sought to specify consequences of urbanism on human personalities. George Simmel in particular made a compelling case for nationality - the dominant characteristic of modern man as a functional adaptation to the overwhelming stimulation and complexities of metropolitan life (Simmel, G. 1950).

An associated concept of modernization was evolved simultaneously. Daniel Learner, introducing the term *"modernization"* for the first time in his study of the middle Eastern societies, refers to the changes brought about in a non-western country by contact, direct or indirect with a western country. To quote him "modernization is the current term for all old process of social change whereby less developed societies acquire the characteristic common to more developed societies" (Learner. D.1964).

Sociologists have not evolved an efficient method of measuring modernisation, as there is no consensus among them regarding the criteria of modernity. However, there has been an agreement among scholars on certain key points qualifying modernization.

D. A. Rustow and R. E. Ward's (1964) measures of modernisation include such specific aspects of changes as:

1. Industrialization of economy and adopting a scientific technology in industry, agriculture, dairy farming, etc. to make them highly productive;

2. Secularization of ideas – that is, a diffusion of secular-rational norms in culture;
3. A remarkable increase in geographic and social mobility, which includes occupational mobility also;
4. A spread of scientific and technical education;
5. A transition from ascribed to achieved status;
6. An increase in material standard of living;
7. High proportion of working force employed in secondary and tertiary rather than primary production, that is manufacturing and services as opposed to agriculture and fishing;
8. An increment of mobility in the society, understood in terms of urbanization, spread of literacy and media participation;
9. High expectancy of life at birth;
10. Relatively greater measure of public participation in the policy as at least democratic representation in defining and choosing policy alternatives.

In brief, for Daniel Learner the modern persons is "an urban literate, who participates fully in the public forum, market place and political arena".

MODERN ATTRIBUTES OF CITIZENS OF SHILLONG

With a view to examine whether the citizens of Shillong consider themselves as modern men/women where the overwhelming majority of the respondents i. e. 87.44 percent said that they were modern.

Self Image of Modern Man

With a view to examine the nature of modernity, we enquired from the respondents as in what way they felt to be modern. Only (87.44 percent) felt that they were modern. From the table (4.1), it is evident that out of them 20 percent of the respondents claimed that it was education which made them to feel so. Exposer to new things (17.67 percent) and scientific outlook (16.74 percent) were the other two opinions of the respondents in this regard. Other responses were individual independence (13.48 percent), acceptance of new ideas (9.76 percent) and upto date fashion (9.76 percent).

The above responses indicate that the Shillongites felt modern because of their education, independence, scientific outlook, exposure to new things, acceptance of new things, ideas and upto date fashion. This has to be seen in terms of their actual behaviour, whether they really perform in their life what they claim.

We enquired from respondents that whether did they wear their traditional dresses or not. To this 70.23 percent of the respondents out of a total of 215 informed that they did not wear their traditional dresses normally, and only 29.76 percent responded that they wore their traditional dresses regularly.

Voluntary organisations play an important role in the lives of modern men living and working in an urban environment. It is here that modern men associate himself with different social clubs. After an enquiry we found that 56.27 percent of the respondents were members of social clubs in the city like the Shillong Club, Young Mens Christian Association, Young Women's Christian Association, Youth Hostel etc.

Table 4.1:
Respondents Opinion About being Modern

RESPONSES	FREQUENCY (215)	PERCENTAGE
Education	43	20.00
Independent	29	13.48
Scientific outlook	36	16.74
Exposure to new things	38	17.67
Acceptances of new ideas	21	9.76
Upto date fashion etc	21	9.76
Not applicable	27	12.55
TOTAL	215	99.94

Source : Field Survey

Attitude to Women and Family

To examine the women's status and what would be the status of women in the society we enquired from the respondents. 37.67 percent of the responses received was that women should respect the traditions and work as per their qualification. They should be completely independent was said by 24.65 percent, women should be treated as equal to men folk was admitted by 18.60 percent which is followed by 10.69 percent who commented that women should continue themselves in the household. The other two options i.e should they rebel against the customs which subordinate them (5.11 percent) and should be completely under the control of their men-folk (3.25 percent) has been responded by very less percentage of the respondents (Table 4.2). Here the opinion differs from both the male and female respondents. But a general view has been taken to present the table, to see how female status or women status is viewed by the general public of Shillong. In case we generalize the data (Table 4.2), the urban Shillong is a mixed bag. While slightly better than half (52.61 percent: sum total of 2, 3, 4 items from Table 4.2) of the respondents emphasized traditional attitudes to the women, 47.35 percent wanted change in women's traditional image. The figure 4.1 below shows the respondents opinion about the Status of Women in the society.

Table 4.2
Respondents Opinion About Status of Women in the Society

RESPONSES	FREQUENCY (215)	PERCENTAGE
Should be completely independent	53	24.65
Should be completely under the control of their men-folk	07	3.25
Should respect the traditions and work as per their qualification	81	37.67
Should continue themselves in the households	23	10.69
Should be treated as equal to men-folk	40	18.60
Should rebel against the customs which subordinate them	11	5.11
TOTAL	215	99.97

Source : Field Survey

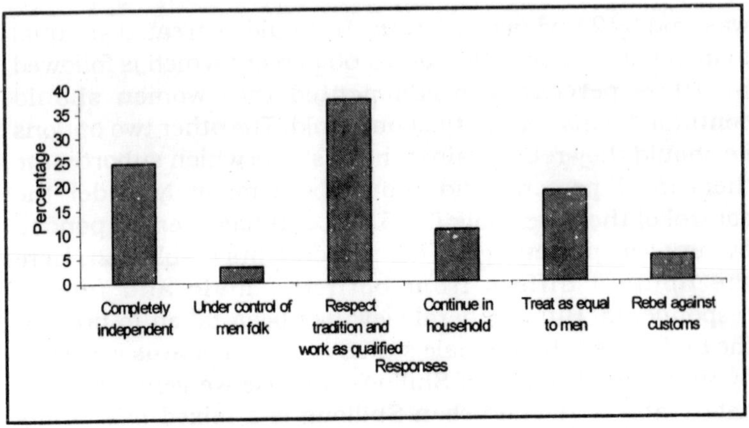

Fig-4.1: Respondents Opinion About Status of Women in the Society

Enquiring from the respondents about the attitudes regarding the recommendation for the women of the household to be the members of any institutions/ associations. In response, we received number of options like any charitable institutions, Women's Club, Ladies Club, Stony Land Club (which is also for the women exclusively) from the respondents. This reflects that the people of Shillong are tradition bound, and they want the women from their household to be members where the association/institution is exclusively for the women.

Regarding the issue of unmarried girls taking jobs outside their home town did startled us, as 73.95 percent of the respondents opted positively. This indeed displays the broad minded attitude of the Shillongites.

To know the broadmindedness and modern attitude of the respondents we have enquired whether they would recommend their daughters to go for modeling / acting in movies. The response we received was that (76.51 percent) were against the opinion of sending their daughters into modeling and acting in movies.

Table 4.3

Number of Children Desired by the Respondent

RESPONSES	FREQUENCY (215)	PERCENTAGE
One	36	16.74
Two	151	70.23
Three	28	13.02
TOTAL	215	99.99

Source : Field Survey

As per the enquiry and data gathered, regarding the number of children a person would like to have during their lifetime, the Shillongites seemed to be alert and educated. From the above table (4.3) it is evident that more than two-thirds of the respondents (70.32 percent) opted for restricting their family to just four members (parents and two issues). Another 16.74 percent and 13.02 percent of the respondents accounted for one and three children respectively. Thus, it is clear that the Shillongites are very concerned about the family size and the restriction of children which is a common phenomena for any modern society. Enquiring about the recommendation of family planning to newly married sons and daughters (183 respondents) which is 85.11 percent, have admitted that they will recommend their views to their children. At the same time all respondents admit to taking proper steps in family planning and have given various suggestions with regard to this subject.

To examine about the maintenance of the family by the people in Shillong city, we enquired from the respondents if they plan for any significant developments for their family and try to achieve them. The responses was that 77.67 percent do some planning for the development of the family and another 22.32 percent admitted that they do not plan for any significant development for their family.

Table 4.4
Respondents Opinion about Significant Development in the Family

RESPONSES	FREQUENCY (215)	PERCENTAGE
Education	85	39.53
Property	43	20.00
Festivals	39	18.13
Not applicable	48	22.32
TOTAL	215	99.98

Source : Field Survey

Similarly we were interested to know the areas where the respondents do the planning and want to achieve it, for their family. The identified areas of the respondents were education (39.53 percent), property (20.00 percent) and festivals (18.13 percent). Therefore it is evident from the above (Table 4.4) that 77.67 percent of the respondents planned for significant development in their family. It is a modern symptom to plan for the future and to achieve it. Thus, as good as 4 of 5 respondents believed in planning for the welfare, such as education for their children, economic well being of their family and celebrating ethnic festivals.

Attitude to Youth and Marriage

Regarding the ideas of the younger generations (53.95 percent) of the respondents are against of having the same ideas as of their parents. This shows that most of the people in Shillong are moving with the phase of modernity and do not believe that the younger generation should have the same ideas as of their parents. Now the view of youngsters are also taken. The children are now no more subordinate and the policy of family is determined according to their wishes. The children now cannot be kept under strict discipline.

To examine the modern youth of Shillong we enquired from our respondents that how do they view the youths of their community. From the responses we received (29.76 percent) said that the youths shirk their responsibilities. 22.79 percent revealed that youths in their community were hard working and competitive. Around 15.34 percent and 14.4 percent respectively have given their views against the youths and said that they were rebels and arrogant. Youths were submissive at 9.30 percent and they continue to be as their elders 8.37 percent were the other two responses which can be seen from Table 4.5 below.

Table 4.5:
Respondents' View about Youths of the Community

RESPONSES	FREQUENCY (215)	PERCENTAGE
They are ignorant	31	14.41
They continue to be as their elders	18	8.37
They are hard working and competitive	49	22.79
They shirk their responsibilities	64	29.76
They are submissive	20	9.30
They are rebels	33	15.34
TOTAL	215	99.97

Source : Field Survey

About the maintaining of social traditions and adopting modern ideas where 44.65 percent of the respondents said that it was possible to do so. And to know in what ways the responses received were like respecting elders, performing religious functions, following cultural trait to mention some.

Table 4.6
Preference for Marital Alliance

RESPONSES	FREQUENCY (215)	PERCENTAGE
Early marriage	00	00
Arranged marriage	16	7.44
Love marriage	98	45.58
Caste / ethnic marriage	21	9.76
Segregation of sexes	39	18.13
Free mixing	41	19.06
TOTAL	215	99.97

Source : Field Survey

With on-set of modernization, the institution of marriage has undergone many changes, and this has been witnessed in Shillong too. We enquired from the respondents about their preferences in marriage. The above table (4.6) indicates that 45.58 percent of the respondents were in the favour of love marriage and 19.06 percent free mixing of the sexes. 18.13 percent felt that segregation of sexes was preferred. The other options of preferences, caste / ethnic marriage (9.76 percent) and arranged marriage (7.44 percent) were reported by a small segment of the respondents. From the above it is seen that most of the people have modern attitude regarding their preference of marriage in Shillong. To know the broadmindedness of the respondents regarding their approval of inter caste / ethnic marriage, 78.60 percent have given positive response which shows that the Shillongites are no more bound with the traditional marriage but have a modern outlook and approve inter caste / ethnic marriage which is found elsewhere in a modern society.

Table 4.7

Modes of choice for Sons/Daughters Marriage

RESPONSES	FREQUENCY (215)	PERCENTAGE
Will give them their choice	65	30.23
Look for the matrimonial advertisement	31	14.41
Consult the family priest and read the horoscope	23	10.69
Take help of the elder kinsmen / women for arranging the alliance	37	17.20
Will do nothing and leave the issue to God	59	27.44
TOTAL	215	99

Source : Field Survey

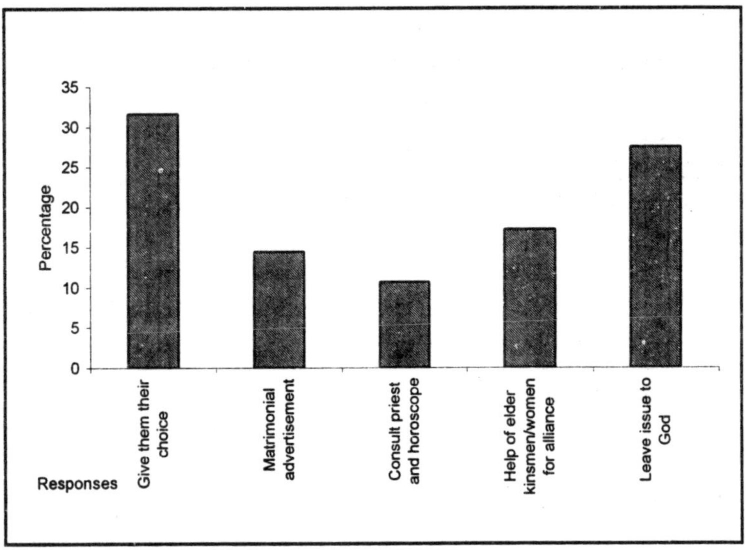

Fig-4.2: Modes of choice for Sons/Daughters Marriage

From the table (4.7) it is seen that nearly one-third of the respondents (30.23 percent) would do nothing regarding their sons / daughters marriage and would give them their own choice, which was followed by (27.44 percent), who would do nothing and leave the issue to God. The other responses were those taking the help of elder / kinsmen / women for arranging the alliance (17.20 percent), those who would look to advertisement (14.41 percent), and the others who would consult their family priests and read the horoscope at 10.69 percent. Thus, as much as (46.13 percent) respondents had a modern attitude regarding the marriage of their sons / daughters. About 27 percent each of them would prefer to leave such affairs in the hands of Gods or priests and elder kinsman. Fig. 4.2.

Attitude to Work, Wealth and Comfort

Possession of Articles of comforts such as car, TV, Computer, Phone etc. does make the person happier, has enquired from the respondents. The responses received was that 62.33 percent said no and the remaining 37.67 percent admitted that the possession of articles of comforts make them happier.

Table 4.8
Criteria of Being Most Successful Individual in Father's Generation

RESPONSES	FREQUENCY (215)	PERCENTAGE
Social Prestige	74	34.41
Religious sanction	30	13.95
Feudal patronage	08	3.72
Economic affluence	53	24.65
Govt. recruitment	47	21.86
Any other	03	1.39
TOTAL	215	99.98

Source : Field Survey

It was interesting to know what were the critieria for the most successful individual in the community during the respondents father's generation. From the above Table (4.8) it is evident that 34.41 percent of the respondents reported for social prestige, 24.65 percent to economic affluence and 21.86 percent to Government recruitment were the other two major responses by the respondents. Religious sanction was another criteria revealed by 13.95 percent of the respondents. The remaining options like feudal patronage and others have been reported by a very small section of the respondents.

Table 4.9
Changing Criteria of Being a Successful Individual in the Community

RESPONSES	FREQUENCY (215)	PERCENTAGE
Social Prestige	42	19.53
Religious sanction	18	8.37
Feudal patronage	12	5.58
Economic affluence	103	47.90
Govt. recruitment	34	15.81
Any other	06	2.79
TOTAL	215	99.98

Source : Field Survey

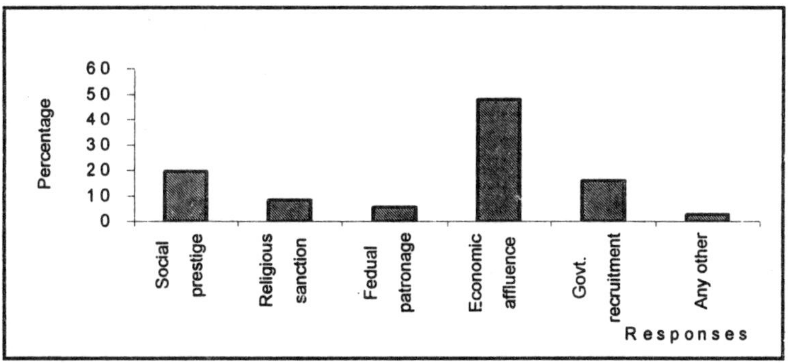

Fig-4.3: Changing Criteria of Being a Successful Individual in the Community

Similarly an enquiry was also made about the criteria for being the most successful individual in the community. It is evident form the above table (4.6) that nowadays economic affluence plays a major role for being the most successful individual which is admitted by 47.90 percent. This has doubled from the previous generation as the most significant attribute. Social prestige at 19.53 percent and Government recruitment at 15.81 percent continued to be the other two major responses, but at the reduced rate (see Table 4.8). Religious sanction, feudal patronage and others have been reported by less than 10 percent each by the respondents. Thus from the above two tables (i.e 4.8 & 4.9) one can see the differences for judging an individual's success in the community. For instance social prestige which was most important during respondents father's generation has undergone great changes. Nowadays it is the economic affluence which is regarded as the most important criteria for judging the individual's success in the society. Which can be also seen from Fig. 4.3.

Every occupation has its own value and status according to nature and standard of work in society. During the ancient period, the teaching profession occupied a very high place in society. When we speak of occupation in the modern term, we classify it under several types like profession, semi-profession, clerical work/shopkeeper, skilled worker etc. It is also said that occupation of the individual is always related to the income which can be both in cash or kind. The status or standard to the individual is also more or less related to income and occupation. In other words income and occupation are the twin characteristics of the economic aspects of an individual's social life.

Table 4.10
Leading Occupations in View of the Respondents

RESPONSES	FREQUENCY (215)	PERCENTAGE
Civil service	03	1.39
Clerical	41	19.06
Teaching	32	14.88
Manual labour	07	3.25
Business leadership	61	28.37
Industry	00	00
Salaried profession like Medico	22	10.23
Independent profession like Law	31	14.41
Journalism	00	00
Whole time politics	09	4.18
Priesthood	08	3.72
Others	01	0.46
TOTAL	215	99.95

Source : Field Survey

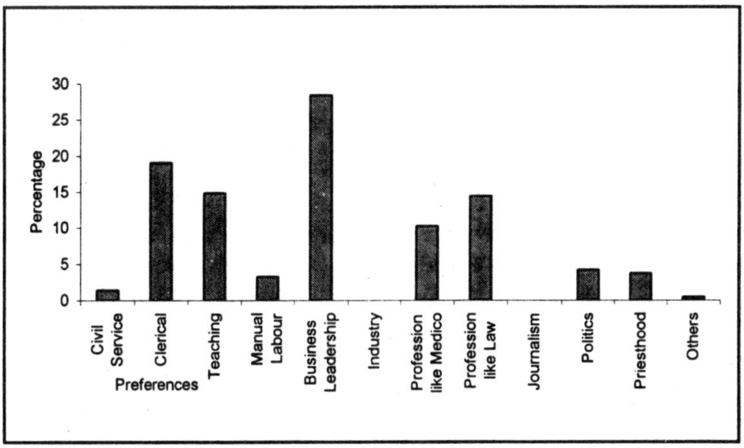

Fig-4.4: Changing Criteria of Being a Successful Individual in the Community

Thus, we were interested to know about the occupational structure prevalent in the city of Shillong. Accordingly we enquired from the respondents regarding some of the leading occupations in Shillong. It is evident from the above table (4.10) that highest number of respondents which is 28.37 percent were of the opinion that business leadership is one of the leading occupation in Shillong. According to 19.06 percent of the respondents clerical rank second, which is followed by Teaching (14.88 percent), independent profession like law (14.41 percent) and salaried profession like medico (10.23 percent) which can also be seen from the above Fig-4.4. The other categories of occupations, like whole time politics (4.18 percent), priesthood (3.72 percent), manual labour (3.25 percent), civil service (1.39 percent) and others (0.46 percent) accounted less than five percent of the responses regarding the leading occupations in Shillong. Journalism and industry was not considered as significant even by a single respondent. More than 45 percent choices were made on salaried vocations, followed by business and law.

Do people face any financial problems in meeting the requirements for their standard of living in Shillong, which is a common phenomenon for any urban place? It has been found out that more than one-third (40.46 percent) of the respondents admitted that their financial position was sufficient to meet the general requirements for the standard of living. 59.35 percent of the respondents admitted that their financial position was not satisfactory to meet the general requirements for the standard of living. This reflects that Shillong is not exception to any other urban place where people are not satisfied with their standard of living. Thus, it is not surprising that none of the respondents from our localities claimed to have travelled abroad for any purpose.

Enquiring about the discipline of the study, which the respondents would like to recommend for their children were in the field of Arts, Science and Commerce. Further enquiry revealed that most of the people would want their children to take up professional courses (e.g . Business Management, Computer Application, Journalism, Field of Technology, Medicine, Tourism, Engineering, Law etc), which were some of the upcoming and more demanding occupations of the day. It is also found out that respondents wanted their sons and daughters to receive education in the State as well as outside the State in order to bring a change in the society by restoring and preserving the rich heritage and traditional values, which they had inherited from the generation gone by.

Orientation towards Politics, Health, Supernatural and Leisure

Political discussion or politics is that subject matter which is a common phenomena of the people of a modern society. Thus, we enquired of the respondents how frequently did they discuss politics with their near and dear ones. From the table (4.11) it is evident that majority of the respondents (50.23 percent) of them regularly discussed politics; 39.06 percent frequently which was followed by 10.69 percent, who rarely discuss about politics. Thus, it is clear that most of the Shillongites discussed politics, and politics plays an important role in their lives.

Table 4.11
Discussion of Politics

RESPONSES	FREQUENCY (215)	PERCENTAGE
Rarely	23	10.69
Regularly	108	50.23
Frequently	84	39.06
TOTAL	215	99.98

Source : Field Survey

It was interesting to know from the respondents what type of newspapers and magazines did they subscribe. The responses differed from one locality to the other. In Jaiaw, the respondents hardly subscribe to any National Newspapers, but read the local newspapers i.e. Mawphor, Rupang, U Peitngor, (Khasi dailies), Shillong Times, Meghalaya Guardian. This is quite the opposite to people living in Laitumkhrah as they were regular subscribers of National Daily's like Hindustan Times, The Statesman, The Asian Age, Times of India, The Hindu etc. The people of Laitumkhrah are also fond of reading magazines such as The Week, Wisdom, Frontline, India Today etc. Thus, one can see the difference between the two localities of Shillong, where one is homogenous and the other is a mixed group area. Seeking further query from the respondents about the reason for their subscribing to national dailies, the reply was that these (Dailies) made them aware of politics, market, world news, entertainment, medical breakthroughs etc. Some of them have also revealed that these papers have helped their children, grand children to keep abreast about the latest/new professions, which are of great demand nowadays.

Table 4.12
Seeking Medical Service by the Respondents

RESPONSES	FREQUENCY (215)	PERCENTAGE
Priest	09	4.18
Tantric	00	00
Vaid/Hakim	25	11.62
Trained Physician	172	80.00
Others	09	4.18
TOTAL	215	99.98

Source : Field Survey

It is interesting to know about the attitude of the people in Shillong regarding the medical facilities they opted for when somebody in the family fall sick. The above table (4.12) gives evidence that 80 percent of the respondents go to trained physicians, when somebody in their family fall sick. Vaid / Hakim is consulted by 11.62 percent, another group consult priests (4.18 percent) and the rest (4.18 percent) go for other means. Thus, it is seen that in Shillong people have the faith in modern health facilities, whereby 80 percent of the respondents go to trained physicians.

Table 4.13
The Criterian which helps one in getting Ahead in Life

RESPONSES	FREQUENCY (215)	PERCENTAGE
Family connections	18	8.37
God's mercy / will	22	10.23
Exposer to scientific knowledge	32	14.88
Membership to an ethnic / caste group	16	7.44
Political patronage	06	2.79
One's ability and Hard work	65	30.23
Ones skill and training	39	18.13
Wealth	17	7.90
TOTAL	215	99.97

Source : Field Survey

From the above table (4.13) it is seen that in Shillong, people had varied options in getting ahead in life. 30.23 percent of the respondents were of the opinion that one's ability and hard work makes an individual to move ahead in life. One's skill and training (18.13 percent) and expose to scientific knowledge (14.88 percent) were the two other major responses given by the respondents. The first three responses together form 63.24 percent and show that the people of Shillong were broad minded and had a modern outlook to the means for getting ahead in life. The other responses which did not have a modern outlook are God's mercy / will (10.23 percent), family connections (8.37 percent), one's wealth (7.90 percent), membership to an ethnic / caste group (7.44 percent) and political patronage (2.79 percent) together forming 36.73 percent. This has been graphically presented in Fig-No. 4.5 below.

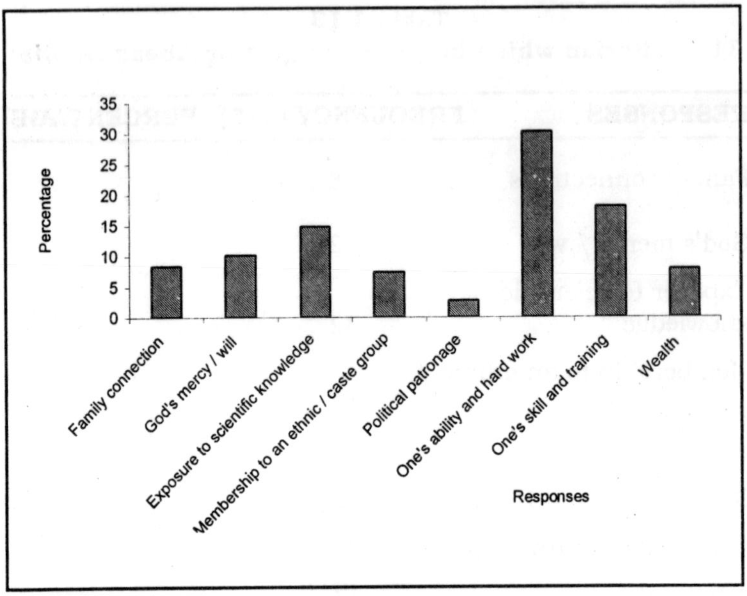

Fig-4.5: The Criterian which helps one in getting Ahead in Life

Table 4.14:
Fuels used for cooking at Home

RESPONSES	FREQUENCY (215)	PERCENTAGE
Gas	111	51.62
Wood	16	7.44
Electricity	53	24.65
Smokeless Chulas	35	16.27
TOTAL	215	99.98

Source : Field Survey

An enquiry was made to know from the respondents what fuels they used at home for cooking. From the above table (4.14) it is evident that more than half of the persons (51.62 percent) use cooking gas as a means of cooking, which was followed by electricity at 24.65 percent. Another 16.27 percent respondents admitted that they used smokeless *chulas*. Cooking by wood was reported by a small section of the respondents i. e 7.44 percent. So, it can be said that with the change to time the people of Shillong were very conscious of their standard of living. Gas, electricity and smokeless *chulas* were may be seen as the outcome of modernization, which had been accepted by the people in the city of Shillong.

Food plays an important role in the individual's life. Religion also has some functions, with the food habit of the people. Thus, we enquired of our respondents what function did food played in their lives or whether it was a matter of habit or choice. The responses received where 93.09 percent of the respondents reported that food was a matter of habit and choice, which showed that religion, tradition by custom had little to do with the matter of odd habit of the people in Shillong. Hence it can be said that people are more empathic regarding food habits, which is a sign of modernity.

Watching movies is a part of entertainment of many people, and also many take movies as a part of their hobby. After an enquiry, we found out that more than 80 percent of the respondents (83.25 percent) watched movies. From the table (4.15) below, 35.81 percent of the respondents watched English movies; followed by 23.30 percent in regional languages and another 18.13 percent watch Hindi movies and the rest (16.74 percent) claimed not to watch any movie. Nearly half of the respondents go to view the movies produced in Indian languages. It is equally significant that more than one third of the respondents watched the movies in English.

Table 4.15
Types of Movies watched by the Respondents

RESPONSES	FREQUENCY (215)	PERCENTAGE
Movies in regional languages	63	29.30
Hindi movies	39	18.13
English movies	77	35.81
Do not watch	36	16.74
TOTAL	215	99.78

Source : Field Survey

Modern equipments play an important role in the lifestyle of the urbanites such as people of Shillong. With a view to understand the extent of their use, we enquired from the respondents what modern equipments were used by them in their home. The response of the question was universally positive as 99 percent of the respondents reported of the use of music system, T. V., refrigerator, washing machine, calculator, wrist-watch, telephone, electric mixture and grinder, V. C. R., camera, internet among the modern equipments. Similarly, we enquired about their urge of the modern equipment that thrill the respondents. It has been found out that most of them replied that motor car, electric oven, digital camera, computer, lap-top thrilled them the most. Thus, it can be said that though the respondents possess some of the modern household consumer equipments; still other equipments which were not in their possession thrilled them. Furthermore, the equipments which thrilled them were of superior technical sophistication.

Table 4.16
Respondents Pattern of Belief

RESPONSES	FREQUENCY (215)	PERCENTAGE
Spirits	51	23.72
Ghost and spirit	43	20.00
Scientific experiments	121	56.27
TOTAL	215	99.99

Source : Field Survey

It was interesting to know that the people of Shillong had their own set of beliefs. From the above table (4.16), it is evident that more than half of the respondents (56.27 percent) believed in scientific experiments. While others believed in the supernatural powers (23.72 percent) and Ghosts and spirits (20 percent). From the above, it is clear that people of Shillong were divided in their views when it came to their set of beliefs.

There is a provision of policing the tribal areas around Shillong under the traditional authorities as per customary laws. Thus, many parts of Shillong urban conglomerate such as Mawlai, Mawroh, Nongthymmai etc. are under traditional authority, and they have the provision of tribal police to control the crime. However, the tribal police is not trained and equipped enough to handle new sets of urban crimes such as smuggling, drug trafficking, extortion etc. As stable traditional tribal society in and around Shillong has tuned into a urban centre, new sets of crimes are very much prevalent.

Table 4.17
Claimed Increase in Types of Crimes in Shillong

RESPONSES	FREQUENCY (215)	PERCENTAGE
Robbery	41	19.06
Rape	20	9.30
Theft	23	10.69
Murder	39	18.13
Extortion	79	36.74
Others	13	6.04
TOTAL	215	99.96

Source : Field Survey

Enquiring about the rate of crime spurt in Shillong compared to the past, all the respondents felt that it is increasing day by day. From the above Table (4.17), it is seen that extortion ranked at the top amongst all other crimes which have been reported by 36.74 percent by the respondents. Next come robbery (19.06 percent) and murder (18.13 percent) respectively, which was followed by theft (10.69 percent). The other categories of crime was reported by less than 10 percent of the respondents. About $2/3^{rd}$ of the crimes (36.74 + 19.06 + 10.69 = 66.49 percent) in Shillong were related to property.

Modernity as a concept has emerged as one of the central themes in social analysis. According to one view, modernity is opposed to tradition, that is to say, what is modern is opposed to tradition. According to other view, all that is traditional is not bad. This ultimately takes us to another dimension of the problem, that is modernity and tradition perhaps can not be exhaustively disclosed in descriptive terms. It has elements of inscription that contain itself. That is why some scholars talk in term of modernization of tradition as well as traditionalism of modernity.

It is often observed that an individual's background plays a significant role in the formation of his attitudes and beliefs. His family, school, neighbourhood, level of education, type of occupation and the income derived there from, all determine to a great extent, the type and quality of his attitudes and values. In other words, we may say that the level of modernity that an individual has acquired in society depends largely on his socio-economic background. Thus, a modern man comes from higher socio-economic status, a family in which members have life opportunities like employment, extra income and education. His reference is not only to the social system of which he is a part, but also to the system external to him: for instance, the city other than his own and the world mass media.

Various scholars have identified the attributes of modernity like Alex Inkeles and David H. Smith (1974), Myron Weiner (1967). But the working definition of modernity which may be applicable to the individual and institutions alike may be defined as – "a temple of science, reason and rationalist, secularism, high aspiration and achievement orientation, overall transformation of attitudes, norms and values, creation of new functional institutions, investment in human resources, a growth oriented economy, a national interest rather than kin, caste, religion, region or language oriented interests, an open society, and a mobile person".

In this connection some of the attributes of modernity are: (i) Empathy, (ii) High participation, (iii) Institutional political participation, (iv) Achievement orientation, (v) Non-tradition attributes to wealth, work, savings and risk-taking, (vi) Faith in the desirability and possibility of change, (vii)

Social, economic and political discipline, and (viii) Capacity to put off immediate and short term satisfaction for higher satisfaction in the long run.

In case, we restrict ourselves to apply this prescription to citizens of our city and its institutions, we have to ask ourselves:

1. Is there a high rate of participation (Social/political/mass media) among the citizens of Shillong?
2. Are the citizens of Shillong achievement oriented? In that case, what have they achieved distinctly as citizens of Shillong?
3. How far do the citizen believe in the non-traditional attitudes to wealth, work, savings and risk taking?
4. Do they have faith in the desirability and possibility of change?
5. Do they have the capacity to put-off immediate and short term satisfaction for higher satisfaction in the long run?
6. Do they empathize with 'others' (ethnic/linguistic/religious/regional groups)?

The answers to the above questions remain anybody's guess. There is a considerable gap between the actual empirical behaviour and expected behaviour of the citizens in Shillong, which may be seen from this chapter already discussed. As long as, this gap between the intentions and peformance is visible and considerable, it is difficult to conclude that city of Shillong is a modern city.

In view of the above, the issue remains unanswered. The citizens of Shillong first of all have to ask themselves in what way, if at all they claim to be, are they modern? Similarly, have we, the citizens of Shillong, given birth to rational – modern institutions to support a future oriented outlook? What ways our cash income, non-traditional job, fashionable western dresses, multi-linguality, friendship across the ethnic divide, new religious alignment, educational degree etc. leads to different approaches to our lives, our attitudes, to others – i.e. individuals and institution? Thus, in order to modernize and to bring about social change in an effective and useful manner, the people will have to inculcate in them a motivation, for achievement. Armed with this motivation they may find a greater incentive to work more and harder for their socio-economic betterment.

This chapter probes the ideas of modernity and modernization of man. Further, it details the modern attributes of citizens of Shillong. We have found that majority of our respondents claimed that they are modern, but when non-conventional opportunities occur, they back out from their committed novel attitudes. For example, issues like allowing their daughters to going for modeling and possibly a career in the films, it is not approved. But our data from this chapter exhibit that people in Shillong are getting influenced by the wave of modern attributes. Still people appear to believe in traditions dear to them and in some cases they are bound by it. Thus, there is a good gap between their belief and performance. The next chapter proposes to discuss the rate of urbanization, urban policies and the State intervention in the affairs of Shillong.

5

URBANIZATION, URBAN POLICIES AND THE STATE

EXPANSION OF SHILLONG IN BEGINNING OF 20th CENTURY

With the dawn of 20th century, urbanization in Shillong had shown a gradual process of growth and change. This was initially due to the partition of Bengal in 1905 and the formation of the new Province of Assam and Eastern Bengal and Shillong was made the temporary headquarters of the same. The process of urbanization had been accelerated by the establishment of new offices along with a group of employees mainly of Bengali middle class origin, gradually settling themselves in different parts of the town. The administrative area came to be known as "civil station" on the Secretariat Hill. The "European Quarters" was on area encircled by Biver Road where the residential quarters for the European officials were located. However, the headquarters of the Provincial Administration was shifted to Dacca in 1910. In 1911, the Colonial Government announced the cancellation of the Partition of Bengal. With this Assam was made the chief Commissioners Province on the 1st day of April 1912. Shillong was again made the capital, but this time it was made the capital of the province of Assam. It was with this revival, more government employees concentrated and settled in Shillong town. Along with government officials penetration of various skilled, semi-skilled and un-skilled, manpower migration was inevitable. The population of Shillong municipality and Shillong urban

Agglomeration i.e. both municipality and cantonment, grew during the first half of 20th century.

Like the Punjabis and Sindhis of North West India, the Bengalis were the victims of political persecution in the wake of partition of the country. Thus, Assam had to accept them and a good number of them were employed in Central establishments like offices of the Accountant General, the Post-Master General and Banks etc. On the other hand, the Assamese population started concentrating in Shillong mainly after the Independence. A small number of people belonging to the affluent class of Upper Assam came to Shillong because of job opportunities and educational facilities. This Community was interested mainly in government jobs rather than in other occupations. Other communities such as Nepali, Marwari, Bihari and also from other states of India gradually started concentrating in Shillong upon urban agglomeration. Therefore, it is not difficult to say that a large number of migrants moved into Shillong seeking livelihood during the colonial regime. It was during this period that the headquarters of the Eastern Command was established and a heavy army influx occurred. Along with the growth of population, trade and commerce expanded to a large extent and more people from various parts of India, particularly enterprising Marwaris, Sindhis and Bengalis felt encouraged to migrate to this urban centre.

There are two types of emigrants in Shillong viz., a group pushed out of the village because of poverty and another group pulled into the city by the attraction of high incomes, job and bright future. The former group although has the tendency to go back to their original villages after a certain period, yet there cannot be seen any decrease in urban population. It is clear from this, that those migrated to Shillong not only joined the urban essential services, and other necessary services, viz., the barbers, cobblers, laundries, masons, scavengers etc. but also to man the colonial bureaucratic set up. The bureaucracy expanded in Shillong after it was declared the capital town of the province of Assam. By 1931, Shillong became the number one town of Assam in terms of population. Expansion of bureaucracy and along with it trade, commerce and education created a condition for the expansion of police force which was one of the pillars of British rule in India. Like other big towns, Shillong too had manifested certain negative aspects of urban life like crime.

The first half of the 20th century witnessed various technological developments in these pristine hill areas. The important among them were the introduction of motor-cars, hydro-electric project and telephone connections. With the installation of telephone and hydro-electric many new offices had come up. During the year 1907-08 a telephone service was installed for the first time in Shillong. Along with the other improvements the education also made its progress intensely during the first half of the 20th century which attracted many people to come in and settle down in Shillong.

Certain important urban characteristics like residential segregation on the basis of race and ethnicity gradually emerged during this period. The Europeans, who were in Government services, preferred the area around Bivar Road and Bishop Cotton Road, where bungalows with extensive lawns and gardens existed. The Khasis remained in areas like Mawkhar, Laban, Jaiaw, Riatsamthiah, Malki, Laitumkhrah, etc. which were their original villages and later came under Shillong Municipality. The significant change took place in these localities was that they became densely crowded with the introduction of modern urban facilities. High officials under colonial government preferred to choose their residential areas in certain places like that of Lachumiere. Various measures were taken to improve drainage and sanitation system. Most of the roads in Shillong were kept remarkably clean. Kutcha drains were replaced by earthenware pipes set in masonary. Inspite of that certain localities like Iewduh (Bara Bazar), Jhalupara areas still need proper sanitation.

Improved medical facilities were introduced during the period of growth under colonial regime. Pasture Institute and Welsh Mission Hospital were established in Shillong after it was made capital of the province of Assam in 1912. Sporadic small-pox was prevalent during the first decade of 20th century. A vaccine depot was maintained at Shillong. The King Edward VII Pasture Institute was and still is one of the most important medical institutions of the century of anti-rabic treatment. Different kinds of vaccines for treatment of disease or for immunization were prepared here. Besides the Civil Hospital, there was an isolation hospital for lepers. The Reid-chest Hospitals was for the treatment of tuberculosis patients and another Government Hospital for the general public, and Ganeshdas was exclusively for women and children. These various medical institutions offered facilities to the urban crowd. However, these facilities were initially meant for the benefit of the colonial rulers which in due course offered facilities to the general masses and this facility was mainly exploited by the urban middle class.

In Shillong, leisure and recreation started on the western model. The British administrators regarded Shillong as one of the lovely Queens of Hill Stations in India. It is also regarded as 'Scotland of the East'. The colonial rulers established the Shillong Club at the heart of Shillong town in 1878. The Golf course of Shillong was regarded as one of the finest in the world. Golf was introduced in Shillong at the turn of 19th century and the present Golf Club was formally opened during the Puja Competitions in October 1924. With the beginning of 20th century various rides were introduced by the British administrators to utilize their past time. The beautiful Ward's Lake amidst the growing town was made in 1893 by Ward, the Chief Commissioner of Assam. The first movie hall in Shillong was Kelvin Cinema near the Shillong Transport Station started in 1921. More and more hotels and restaurants were coming up. All these had given urban characteristics to Shillong during the colonial period.

Thus, during the period1901 to 1951, Shillong had shown a gradual growth as town within the colonial limitations. It was the inclusion of Khasi Hills in the map of British India, the decision to make Shillong the capital of Assam was a major decisive factor that helped the growth of Shillong. Therefore, it is not very difficult to argue that the process of urbanization in modern sense was set to a motion by exogenic factor. With the departure of the British rulers and arrival of representative government, the political scene of Shillong changed the social, economic and political milieu of the tribal society in a more significant way. There was only one town i.e., Shillong Municipality in Meghalaya upto 1931. It was in 1931 that Shillong cantonment was declared a town. There was no change in the number of towns during the colonial period and even upto 1951. Two more new towns, Nonthymmai and Mawlai were added in 1961 census.

The 1981 census shows a significant growth in the number of urban centres in Meghalaya. Six more new towns were declared in 1981 census. Out of these six new urban centres, two, viz., Pynthorumkhrah and Madanrting are extensions of the Shillong urban agglomeration. These two new towns infact, signify the urban expansion of Shillong itself. Thus urbanization in Shillong has been usually rapid during the recent period. It is also important to note here that the recently recorded significant growth of urbanization in Shillong was mainly due to the expansion of administrative machinery i.e. bureaucracy in the different parts of this traditionally tribal region. This bureaucratic expansion has been rapid after independence and more particularly after the creation of Meghalaya as a State in the Indian Union. In Shillong the bureaucracy expanded in such a way that the impact of the shifting of the capital of Assam from Shillong to Guwahati was not felt much. The vacuum created by the shifting of the capital of Assam was immediately filled up by the expansion of bureaucracy in Shillong, establishment of North Eastern Hill University, North Eastern Council, North Eastern Electrical Power Corporation and other Central Government establishments.

The urban scheduled tribes of Shillong include local tribal people as well as various other hill tribes viz., the Mizos, the Nagas, the Manipuris, the Arunachalis etc. The non-tribal migration seems to be concentrating mostly in Shillong municipality, Shillong cantonment and Nongthymmai areas, whereas Mawlai and other small towns of Shillong possess only a minimum number of non-tribals. The non-tribal migrants prefer places which could provide them with enough prospects. Prospects does not mean only job prospective, but also educational, medical and recreational facilities. Thus it can be observed that non-tribals prefer to dwell mostly in central Shillong and nearby surroundings. However, newly declared town Mawlai has a very large number of scheduled tribe population because it was already thickly populated Khasi village and gradually developed into a town.

The importance of trade and commerce grew simultaneously with the process of urbanization. Besides the markets at smaller urban centres, Shillong has been functioning as the only important central market. During the last two decades the importance of this market grew further. Shillong became second only to Guwahati as the distributing centre for the North-East India. Supply of various commodities to Cachar, Tripura and Mizoram is done through Shillong. Among the outgoing products potatoes, vegetables, fruits, forest produces, timbers, lime-stone, cement and coal are important. The incoming commodities are food-grains, textile, iron, steel, hardware materials, consumer good, seasonal fruits and vegetables, machinery and machinery parts, etc.

GROWTH OF POPULATION

Shillong town is an overgrown village. The population of Shillong has increased at a rapid pace leading to acquisition of new settlements under urban areas. Similarly, the share of workers in traditional non primary occupations has declined to a great extent adding more to their existing urban characteristics.

Thus, in 1931, an Urban Agglomeration was formed in the state capital with Shillong municipality and Shillong cantonment as constituent units. In 1961, two more towns, viz. Nongthymmai and Mawlai were added and expanded the area of Shillong Urban Agglomeration (UA). In 1981, two more towns known as Pynthorumkhrah and Madanrting were added to the Shillong (UA). Thus, increasing the total number of the constituents units of Shillong (UA) to 6 numbers. There is no new town in 1991 census. In the 2001 census a new town known as Nongmynsong has come up and formed a new constituent units of Shillong (UA). Although 7 towns including Shillong municipality constitutes an Urban Agglomeration. The constituent towns are Mawlai, Nongthymmai, Madanrting, Pynthorumkhrah, Nongmynsong, Shillong (municipality) and Shillong cantonment (Map 5.1). There is only one Urban Agglomeration with 7 constituent towns in the state in 2001. Shillong municipality is the core town of urban agglomeration. The total population of Shillong Urban Agglomeration is 2,67,881 persons with 1,4,416 males and 1,33,465 females.

Map 5.1

SHILLOGN

URBAN AGGLOMERATION, 2001

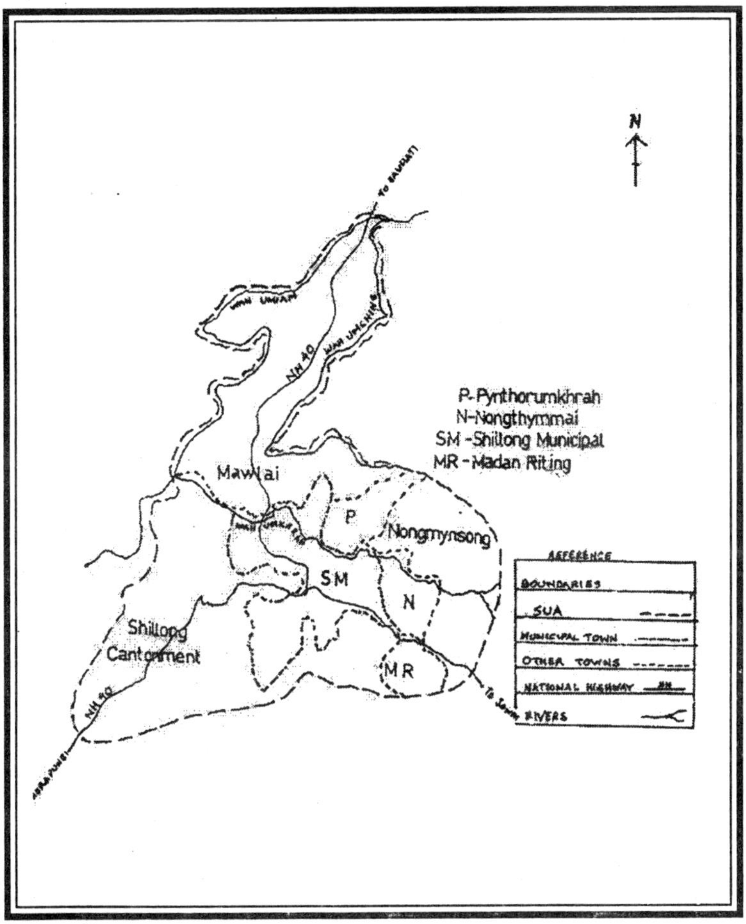

Source: Survey

Table 5.1
Population Growth of Shillong Municipality

Year	Persons	Decadal Variation(+)	Decadal Variation (P.C)
1901	9621	—	—
1911	13639	+4018	+41.76
1921	17203	+3564	+26.13
1931	26536	+9333	+54.25
1941	38192	+11656	+43.93
1951	58512	+20320	+53.20
1961	72438	+13926	+20.80
1971	87659	+15221	+21.01
1981	109244	+21585	+24.62
1991	131719	+3894	+20.57
2001	132876	+19638	+0.88

Source : Census of India.

Table 5.1 shows the distribution and growth of population within Shillong municiplaity ward-wise. Population of Shillong municipality has grown from a mere 9,621 in 1901 to 1,31,719 in 1991, roughly 13 times in 90 years. This may look impressive but as events of last two decades indicate it is not as spectacular as witnessed in many similarly placed cities even within the region. One reason for this has been cited as under-reporting during the decadal censuses. The other is that largest part of the growth is accounted for in the adjacent townships and also areas that have became urbanised but are still classified as rural and are not included within the municipal jurisdictions.

The population of Shillong municipal area as on 1st March 2001, is 1,32,876 which is only 19,738 persons more than 1991 census having a growth rate of 0.88 percent during 1981-1991 having more than 3.56 percent. The population of Shillong (M) as per 1991 census shows that the growth rate during the decade 1991-2001 is the lowest when compared with the earlier decades. In Shillong municipal area there is no further scope for expansion of residential housing pattern.

Population Growth of Shillong Urban Agglomeration

The population of Shillong (UA) as on 1st March 2001 is 26,7881 and the decadal growth rate during 1991-2001 is 19.93 percent. The growth rate of the State population of Meghalaya during the decade 2001 is only 29.94 percent, which is less by merely 3 percent from the last decade which was at 32.86 percent. East Khasi Hills District which is having the largest number of population among all the districts of the State with a population of 6,60,994 as per 2001 census, shows the lowest rate with 22.88 percent. On the other hand, Shillong (M) is the core town of Urban Agglomeration. The total population of Shillong (UA) for both males and females is 1,34,416 and 1,33,465 respectively. The comparative population growth of Shillong during 1991-2001 is shown in (table 5.2) below.

Table 5.2
Comparative Population Growth of Shillong

City/District/ State	Population in Number		Decadal Growth Rate.	
	2001	1991	1991-2001	1981-91
1. Shillong (M)	1,32,876	1,30,691	0.88	+19.63
2. Shillong (U.A)	2,67,881	2,22,273	19.93	+27.23
3. East Khasi Hills Dist.	6,60,994	6,57,160	22.88	+28.50
4. Meghalaya	23,06,069	17,74,778	29.94	+31.80

Source: Census of India.

Sex Ratio of Shillong Urban Agglomeration

As per 2001 census, the sex ratio of the State is 975 as against 955 in 1991. Sex ratio has gradually declined over the decades. The gradual increase in the sex considerable improvement of the sex ratio has been noticed in census 2001 as compared to 1991 census. The decadal variation of sex ratio during 1991-2001 is highest in the East Khasi Hills District. While comparing the sex ratio of the different districts with that of the State sex ratio, East Khasi Hills has the highest sex ratio of the State average. Meghalaya is at rank 7 in terms of sex ratio among the Indian States with regards to Shillong (M) area the total number of females as per 2001 census is 66,747 and males is 66,129 in numbers. In Shillong Agglomeration the number of females is 1,33,464 and males 1,34,416 numbers. The difference of population by sex is 951. (Table 5.3) below shows the sex ratio of Shillong Urban Agglomeration.

Table 5.3
Sex Ratio of Shillong Urban Agglomeration

Name of U.A	1961	1971	1981	1991	2001
Shillong U.A	762	855	902	888	993
Mawlai	960	938	905	870	1,077
Nongthymmai	852	881	912	944	1,077
Madanrting	-	-	950	955	970
Shillong(M)	785	765	762	765	752
Shillong Cant.	466	765	762	765	752
Pynthorumkhrah	-	-	867	863	942
Nongmynsong	-	-	-	-	917

Sources: Census of India

Present Trends

During the last three decades or so the city has undergone a radical transformation from a hill resort to a multifunctional service centre, catering to a host of administrative and other service functions not only for the State but for the entire North East Region, comparable next to Guwahati. From a small village in 1866 to a class-I city in 2001, the city has grown to cater to the needs of the state as an enclave of modernization in the midst of the rural-tribal hinterland that continued without any significant change. The modern transport network and expansion of the city infrastructure have influenced the tribal social order but only to a limited extent thereby giving rise to a dualistic economic organisation.

With the increase in the population, urban expansion of Shillong has taken heavy toll on the forests. Many localities have come up in forest clearings and urban invasion has engulfed steep forested slopes. Localities like Kench's Trace, Bishnupur,Lumparing, Alugodown, Laitkor, Rynjah have come up in clearings of upland forests. While city has outgrown to occupy isolated places, forest clearings and even steep slopes in all directions under increasing population pressure, open space, stream beds, and steep stream banks have been encroached upon within the central localities. Today Shillong is expanding at a very fast rate and taking within its ambits the peripheral areas.

Thus, urbanization is spreading rapidly in Shillong and its population is becoming more cosmopolitan in nature which is not only affecting the social condition but the economic life style of the people. We thereby see in Shillong of the present decade a repetition of the processes of the earlier decades when the little civil station so reminiscent of the colonial outpost of the British. Due to its varied functions and high rate of urbanization the population of Shillong has increased at a rapid pace. This resulted to development of new settlements under urban areas.

STATE URBAN POLICIES

Meghalaya being an autonomous area under the Sixth Schedule of the Indian Constitution, the management and administration of land of greater part of the State is under the jurisdiction of Autonomous District Councils. As regards legislation on town and county planning, Meghalaya adopted the Assam town and county planning Act, 1959 and the same has been extended to the entire state in January,1989. There were practically no legislation in operation during 1972-1989, the period during which huge amount of Public Investments made. This is perhaps one of the reasons for haphazard growth of Shillong. This Act allows for setting up of an

Advisory Council and Development Authorities for the implementation of Master Plans and Development Schemes. These provisopms along with Municipality, Public Work Department, Public Health Engineering Department, The Meghalaya Housing Board, Urban Affairs Department, District Council and other agencies engaged in various development works in urban area with their respective approach and lack of co-ordination and integration, the very purpose of an integrated and overall planned development of the urban area is defeated.

Though Shillong Municipality as constituted under the Assam Municipal Act 1955 and is expected to take up various schemes of urban development, it is severely handicapped by a weak resource base and absence of adequate sources of revenue like Octroi etc. Although the Municipality is empowered to collect the taxes and fees on house, water, lighting tax, market fees, service charges on central government buildings, vehicle entry tax, car parking, trade license fee, rent on land and houses, stalls and shops etc. It has been suggested by Government that its only major source of revenue is in the form of Government grants and loans. Apart from this, municipality is also handicapped by an inefficient and over staffed administrative set up which is engaged in primarily maintenance of services like town roads, water supply, drainage etc.

Shillong with nearly 2.50 lakhs of population and municipal administration covering only 50 percent of urban population can not plan for the whole urban area in an integrated manner. The civic affairs and investment are still managed by the traditional local bodies in other parts of Shillong and investments are made by various departments of State Government. Meghalaya Urban Development Authority which has been constituted under the Meghalaya Town and Country Planning Act, 1973 (Assam Town and Country Planning Act, 1959 as adopted by Meghalaya) and started functioning in March, 1990 is also dependent on Government grants for its survival as it has no source of revenue at present. The Authority has to consider other sources of revenue like fees from building permissions and also through service charges from channelisation of funds to government agencies for urban development schemes and through creation of assets.

The Meghalaya Transfer of Land (Regulation) Act, 1971 as passed by the Assembly received the assent of the President on the 28th December, 1971 under section 3(i) of this Act-"no land in Meghalaya shall be transferred by a tribal to another non-tribal except with the previous sanction of the Competent authority". Because of this Act, transaction of land has become difficult and artificial scarcity of houses has been created. To solve the problem of housing, it is imperative to revise this Act. For example, the Department of Urban Affairs has prepared a master plan for Shillong covering an area of nearly 104 square kilometers. 90 percent of this master plan area is outside the jurisdiction of the Municipal Board. This has created unique problems for the administration in providing infrastructure and other facilities in the areas whereby in one shot they may create assets, but cannot sustain the benefits out of it.

Thus, for proper land use management of urban area, the existing bodies should be strengthened, their jurisdiction may be extended where ever necessary and new boards should not be set up. These boards should function efficiently and should make attempts to mobilise addition resources for providing the desired level of services to the rate payers. It is suggested that a master plan should be prepared for long term planned development of the city.

Existing Land Use

Quality of urban life and functional efficiency of a town is dependent on proper disposition of activities and inter-relationship it offers between the different activities. In order to understand and analyse systematically the functional relationship between various usages of work, living and recreational areas, a detailed land use survey was conducted by the Urban Affairs Department. This land use survey has also helped in identifying the incompatible activities influencing city life functions. While the detailed land use analysis of the inhabited areas reflect the problem of inadequacy of urban land for various uses, the similar analysis of the planning area presents the picture of available land resources. Remedy to most of the problems of Shillong lie in organizing pattern of land uses in the city.

The Shillong Master Plan covers an area of 17,400 hectares of which 5494.10 hectares or 31.58 percent of the total area is developed area. 1,573.88 hectares or 9.04 percent of the total area is undevelopable owning to excessive slope and height of land; 803.07 hectares or 4.62 percent of the total area is under urban agriculture and 4451.93 or 21.58 percent is under forest and water bodies. Of the total master plan area, 5077.02 or 29.18 percent is developable area. (Table 5.4) shows the land resources within the Master Plan Area.

Table 5.4
Land Resources-Shillong Master Plan

Sl. No.	Land use	Area (in hectares)	Percentage to total area
1.	Developed area	5494.10	31.58
2.	Undevelopable area	1573.88	9.04
3.	Developable area	5077.02	29.18
4.	Urban Agriculture	803.07	4.62
5.	Forests and water bodies	4451.93	25.58
	Total area	17400	100.00

Source: Directorate of Urban Affairs.

Slums

The emergence of slum in Shillong is mainly due to accelerated high growth rate and unplanned physical development. The pace and magnitude of inter-state migration capitulated with an influx from outside the state has left the authorities concerned, lagging behind in providing the resources to meet the basic amenities and thereby the number of slum dwellers are increasing over the years. There are 23 slums pockets identified within the master plan area with an estimated 76,730 dwellers during 1991.

Since the land is owned by private individual except 3.02 sq. km within the municipal area, most of the slums are developed in private land. Only in Jhalupara within cantonment area and sweeper lane (at present the land is under possession of the Municiapl Board) slums have developed. In the absence of the proper development control or regulation, indiscriminate plot subdivision and disposal for development devoid of proper provision for access, services and disposal system leading to the growth of slum, degrading the living environment. On the other hand, as stated earlier, portion of houses without having sufficient kitchen or toilet facilities are rented to number of families in the same unit. In area like Lumparing, Demsieniong, Malki, Madan Laban, Riat Laban, Lower Mawprem, Wahingdoh, Wahthapbru etc., most of the slum dwellers are having their own land and houses. In Barapathar, Qualapatti and Pynthorumkhrah, etc., the maximum slum dwellers are in private rented houses.

The main problems of slums in Shillong are (i) lack of basic civic amenities such as approach lane and water supply, drainage, lighting and sanitary facilities, (ii) overcrowding, both in terms of space density and occupied residential unit, (iii) unliveable housing units, (iv) unemployment and under employment accompanied by, (v) deprivation of educational facilities and health contingencies.

Slum improvement

There was no legal backing outside the normal wards for enforcing and implementing slum improvement works as the Meghalaya Slum Area (Improvement and Clearance Act) 1973 was extended over the whole State only in January, 1990. However, the problems of existing slums and growth of new ones endangering health's, hygiene and environment of the city had drawn the attention of the authorities to ensure in improving the degrading environmental condition. The Urban Affairs Department started the slum improvement works way back in 1974-75 and continuing doing so under environmental improvement of urban slum scheme by way of providing physical amenities. In the process 13 slum area were fully covered but the benefit could not be sustained due to lack of follow-up action. However, the impact on overall development could not be achieved as the scheme partially took care of one of the problem area i.e. public physical amenities where as the individual dwelling units which required improvement left untouched and the human aspect were neglected. Hence, to facilitate these aspect the department has introduced the Urban Basic Services scheme as well as Nehru Rozgar Yojana in these slum areas. These schemes takes care of both social input such as health care and health facilities for the vulnerable section i.e., the children and women nutrition, pre-school learning, adult literacy, upgradation of housing units, etc, as well as economic upliftment by way of providing job opportunities through wage employment, enhance and impart skill and facilitate finance for entrepreneurship which will augment the family income.

State Housing Policy

Recognising the importance of housing, the State Government has created a full fledged housing department right from its inception to promote and facilitate the housing stock in the state. The housing department undertakes construction of residential houses as well as provides financial assistance to individuals for construction of houses. However, due to the resource constraints it could not achieve the desired results. Hence, for channelizing institutional finance a State Housing Boards was set up in 1985. Inspite of the involvement of various agencies it could not cope up with the increasing demand. Hence, to make concerted effort in this direction the State Government has introduced the Meghalaya State Housing Policy in 1988, which lays emphasis on increasing the housing stock and qualitative upgradation of the existing shelters by way of providing necessary construction material at subsidised rate and soft loan for the poorer section of the people. The main emphasis is to encourage private individuals and co-operatives for owing the houses. Therefore, a more comprehensive approach has to be adopted to encourage the private sector in increasing the housing stock to meet the demand of all sections of the people.

The future expansion in urban activities will lead to increased demand for housing. Assuming a household size of 5 persons, it has estimated that an addition of 40,060 housing units has to be added to the existing housing stock to accommodate the additional population out of this, by 2001 A.D. 17,550 additional units will be required. Besides, it is estimated that approximately 8,000 units (20 percent of the existing housing stock) requires up-gradation/ improvement to become habitable units. Keeping in view the above additional stock the additional space required for gross residential use will be 1457 hectares with a gross density 30 to 40 persons per acre. It is assumed that around 75,000 persons will be absorbed within the Urban Agglomeration within the Master Plan Area.

The task of adding up another 40,060 dwelling can be achieved only by combine effort made by both the Government agency and private sector. The role of Government agency to mitigate the future housing demand requires a greater thrust. In order to encourage private sector, it is very much essential to provide suitable and developed land for housing by the Government agencies at the initial stage. The necessity of rental housing in case of Shillong can never be under-played till near future due to the provision of the existing land Transfer Act as well as the land owner ship system. Hence attempts should be made to encourage private sector in this direction by way of providing loans for the purpose at the same terms and interest as for individual ownership.

Although the National Housing Policy, as well as State Housing Policy, envisage extending required finance for housing, it will be an upheaval task for the authorities concerned to arrange huge quantum of finance required within 2011 A.D. Even if 25 percent of the future housing demand will be taken up by people out of their own resources, 30,000 dwelling units are to be financed within 20 years. Hence concerted efforts should be made to finance from housing financial institutions, such as H. U. D. CO., L.I.C., G. I. C., H. F. D. C., and recently initiated National Housing Bank. Added to this, housing co-operatives should be encouraged.

COMMUNITY FACILITIES AND URBAN SERVICES

(i) Community Facilities

Education

Shillong has become an important educational centre

not only for the state but for the whole north eastern region. The establishment of the North Eastern Hill University has added to the importance of Shillong as an educational centre. The town has sufficient number of educational institutions to serve the present population. But with the increase in population there will be need to create some more educational facilities. Within the standard urban area, there are 88 Primary Schools, 49 Junior Secondary and Middle Schools, 56 High Schools, 10 Colleges, 20 Vocational Institutions and 1 University but they are not uniformly distributed over the entire area. Besides, there is also one Polytechnic Institution and two Industrial Training Institutions catering to the need of the state population. Shillong did not have facilities for medical sciences, engineering and other specialised courses. It is felt necessary that these branches of studies be set up to cater to the need of the state population and in fact a modest beginning has been made in private sector.

Health

Shillong town has the maximum number of medical facilities in the Khasi Hills District. People from all over the district come to Shillong for their medical requirements. However the town lacks in facilities of specialised medical services. Till 1981, according to Directorate of Urban Affairs, there were seven hospital, one family planning centre, ten dispensaries, one T.B. Clinic and one maternity and Child Welfare Centre.

Recreation

Compared to many hill towns of India, Shillong probably can boast of having more recreational facilities. The Golf Course at Polo Ground is one of the best in Asia where important competitions are held every year. The Polo Ground and the Garrison Ground provided facilities for out door sports. Besides the famous Ward's Lake, the Lady Hydari Park, various Waterfalls, a Botanical Garden and a lot of pine forest provides acute recreational facilities to the inhabitants of the town.

Social and Cultural Facilities

The town has a number of Clubs and Community halls spread over the town. There is also a Central Library run by the Government. There are five cinema halls located mostly in the central area of the town. The town also has a stadium located in Polo Ground. Besides, there are a few organised sports centre located at different areas of the town. As far as places of worship are concerned the town has adequate number of Churches, Mosques and Temples.

Future proposals

Education

As per the planning norms and standards laid down by the committee on plan projects (capital) and town and country planning organisation (TCPO) one college for a population of 1.50 lakhs has been proposed. Taking this into consideration, Shillong does not require additional colleges till the end of the plan period. However, seeing the growing demand, one college has been proposed towards the north eastern side of the Master Plan Area. It is felt that this college will cater to the needs of the people living in and around that area. As regards High Schools, it has been prescribed that for every 10,000 population, one high school is required. Shillong at present has 56 high schools. However, for the additional population of 1.50 lakhs to be accommodate in the north eastern side of the Master Plan Area, 12 high school with facilities for middle schools has been proposed.

Health

Even though Shillong has a number of medical facilities, the town lacks in specialised Medical Services and patient have to go outside the state for their medical treatment. In view of this, it is proposed that a specialised hospital having all modern facilities is set up in the proposed Regional Institute of Medical Sciences. This will go a long way in solving the medical needs not only of the town but the region as a whole.

Recreation

The plan proposes that more open spaces and play ground are created all over the Master Plan Area. Further, with the Government's policy of attracting more tourists to Shillong, the recreational facilities must be augmented and diversified, providing special attention of fishing, boating, hiking, golf, etc. Besides absence of proper picnic spots for the Shillong people is felt badly, when there are plenty of spot which can be cheaply developed for the purpose.

Social and Cultural Facilities

It is proposed that community halls be set up in each major locality to create a better social and physical environment. It is proposed that the community buildings be so planned and designed so as to provide adequate space facilities which could be organised for different individual groups for social and cultural activities. Community halls should also include indoor games and library.

(ii) Urban Services

Water Supply

Most hill towns face acute problem of water supply during the dry season. This is because the water supply in most hill towns is by and large governed by rainfall. Sources of water supply in hills are generally rivers, lakes, springs, natural falls and streams. The water from these sources are fed directly in the piped distribution system and stored in tanks where it is distributed to the consumers through piped water supply.

When the municipality was first set up in 1910 the population of Shillong was 10,000 only and the sources from which water was supplied to 10,000 population was Wahjalnoh, Wahrisa and Madan Laban. With the constant growth of population, the Government through the Public Health Engineering explored Umkhen source and replenished the supply, though the position did not show any remarkable improvement. Again the Public Health Engineering implemented two schemes namely Umjasai and Crinoline but still there was no perceptible improvement as the sources were gradually drying up during the lean months.

The responsibility of supply of portable water within the municipal limits rests with the Shillong Municipality Board where as in the other township within the Shillong Urban Agglomeration and the other rural settlements it is being managed by the Public Health Engineering Department.

1.25 lakhs gallon per day is available from Umkhen, which is tapped by P.H.E. Department. Hence the total quantum of water available to the Shillong Municipal Town is only 19.37 lakhs gallon per day. Within the installation of the Greater Shillong Water Supply Scheme (Phase I) the water scarcity within the Shillong Urban Area has been relieved to some extent. At present a regular supply of 17 lakh gallon per day is maintained by the Public Health Engineering Department.

2.85 lakhs gallons of treated water is distributed from Umkhen water supply scheme to different areas of Nongthymmai and Laitumkhrah. With Umsohlang as the source, 3.00 lakh gallons of treated water is pumped to different areas of Mawlai town. Hence the total quantum of water available within the Shillong Urban Areas is 25.22 lakh gallon per day which is much below the desired requirements.

Taking into account a minimum of 100 litres per head per day the total requirement of water within the Shillong urban agglomeration by 1991 works out to be 4.8 MGD per day and by the end of the plan period, i.e., 2011 it will go up to 7.9 per day. Whereas within the master plan area the present requirement is 6.4 MGD per day and by 2011 it will go up to 10.8 MGD per day. However, the Public Health Engineering has estimated that by 2006 the ultimate supply of water, works out to be 8.40 MGD, which means a total deficiency of 2.40 MGD by 2011. It is proposed that the concerned departments must explore the possibilities of more sources around Shillong so that the scarcity of water supply can be overcome in the long run.

Power Supply

The Shillong Hydro Electric Company Limited was started in 1922 and after operating for about 55 years, was taken over by the Meghalaya Electricity Board in 1977. Since the take-over of the supply unit, considerable improvement has been made by Meghalaya State Electricity Board to meet the growing power demand. The present peak demand in the city is more than 20 MVA and the whole network if properly designed and strengthened with adequate metering arrangements should enable the Board to earn substantial revenue.

The present source of supply of power is from the 132 KV grid sub-station at Mawlai. Even though the power supplied at present is adequate yet poor conditions are experienced in many areas as during peak and off peak hours. This is due to many technical defects. As regards street lighting the present schemes are implemented by the Meghalaya State Electricity Board with funds released by the Urban Affairs Department and Shillong Municipal Board. Outside the Shillong Municipal areas, the Government sanction funds for installation and maintenance of mercury and sodium vapour lamps.

The present power supply catering to the need of Shillong require renovation and augmentation not only to meet the present demand of the consumers but at the same time should be able to meet the requirements of the ever increasing population. Meghalaya being surplus in power should take the initiative in having a properly designed distribution system for Shillong to give better services to its consumers and at the same time earn more revenue to improve the financial position of the Board. The power requirement by 2011 works out to be 50 MVA within the Master Plan Area. Hence an addition of 30 MVA has to be added to the existing supply system. It is proposed that new distribution lines and sub-stations are set up in the new township to meet the future demand.

Sewage and Sewage Disposal System

At present the town has no integrated sewage system. The town, especially the areas falling outside the Municipal limits are dominated by latrines where the discharge falls directly to the open drains or streams causing pollution. It is obvious that Shillong requires an underground sewage system to check pollution. It is felt that it will not be possible to lay sewage lines in the thickly built up areas as this will call for considerable demolition. In view of this it is proposed that the latrines be converted into sanitary latrine as an alternative to the sewage system, in the existing built up areas. As regards the proposed built up areas, it is necessary to construct underground sewage facilities and the main line should be connected to a treatment plant before being discharged to the streams.

Other services: Post and Telegraph

There is one main Post and Telegraph Office located

within the Secretariat complex. Besides, there are a number of branch and Sub-Post Office located in different areas of the town. It is felt that a few more Sub-Post Offices are needed to cater to the need of the entire Master Plan.

Police Station

The town is served by a main Police Beat Houses located in different parts of the town. But with the growth of population, it is felt that some more Police Beat Houses and Police outposts has to be set up to cater to the need of the entire Master Plan.

Fire Service

The town is served by two fire fighting service. It is proposed that the fire fighting service should be located at strategic locations throughout the Master Plan area in such a manner so that they reach the effected spots in the short possible time.

Burial and Cremation Ground

The town has a sufficient number of burial and cremation grounds to serve the future population. But it is felt necessary that the burial and cremation ground needs to be improved and properly maintained. As regards cremation grounds it is proposed that the existing cremation grounds which follow the traditional system should be replaced by electric crematorium.

Trade and Commerce

With increasing population commercial activities in Shillong has expanded considerably. Shopping activities has grown tremendously within the town area. Iewduh (Barabazar) and Police Bazar continues to be the biggest wholesale and retail market respectively in the whole state whereas other shopping centres like Laitumkhrah, Polo Bazar, Laban, Malki serves the neighbourhood population. However, there is a serious shortage of warehousing and storage facilities particularly for goods of perishable nature.

Most of the wholesale activities of the city ranging from food grains to machineries are located at Iewduh. It acts a a collection and distribution point for agro-based products. The bulk of commodities are transacted on the same day even in a distress sale as there is no cold storage and adequate ware housing facilities available nearby. Besides its wholesale activities, it serves as a major retail centre of the city. However, the areas in and around Iewduh is overcrowded and there is hardly any scope of its expansion. Hence, efforts has to be made to decentralise some of the functions to release congestion and to channelise the activities to facilitate its growth. Recently, an organised whole sale market centre has been initiated at Mawiong.

The main wholesale and retail centre at Iewduh is congested and completely saturated with commercial activities. The nearby areas of Paltan Bazar and Mawlonghat has also developed intensively resulting in traffic congestion and degradation of the environment. It is therefore necessary that both wholesale and retail activities are decentralised and shifted to suitable areas within the Master Plan boundary.

At present, Iewduh and Police Bazar are the main retail centres and caters to the need of the entire city. In addition, there are retail markets at Polo, Laitumkhrah, Laban, Dhankheti etc. It is proposed that some more retail markets at Umpling, Mawlai, Bishnupur and Nongthymmai, are to be set up. As regards local centres, it is proposed that each residential area will have its own local shopping centre.

Industry

Industrially, Shillong has not made headway though there is enough potential for development of cottage and small scale industries in and around Shillong urban areas. The existing industries are haphazardly located mainly along the major traffic arteries thereby creating traffic congestion and various other problems. At present there is only one organised industrial area near the meter factory. It may however be necessary to create an industrial base for Shillong town in view of the fact that wider economic activities may have to be created to cater to and sustain the ever increasing population of the town.

Administration

The central areas of Shillong i.e., the areas around I. G. P., Barik, Lower Lachumiere etc. – are better known as the

Secretariat complex is considered as the most important administrative centre not only for the city, but the region as a whole. Here in are located the important State level offices, District level offices and Regional level offices like the North Eastern Council, the Accountant General's Office, the Meghalaya Secretariat and the Additional Secretariat, General Post Office, the Deputy Commissioner's Office and numerous other State and District level Offices. This area in fact is the administrative hub of the entire region. Besides various other State level, District level and Regional level offices are scattered throughout the Shillong city.

It has been observed that high rate of administrative activities are taking place in the city. Various State and Central Government offices, Autonomous Bodies, Banks and Business establishments have extended their functions within the core area of the city. The above organisations have been expanding in the last few years and there has been no attempt to effectively decentralised them away from the core areas, and since most of the offices are occupying residential houses on rent there is a steady increase in the rent structure, besides creating shortage in residential houses.

It is presumed that administrative activities is most likely to increase at the rate of state population, employment is also likely to increase with the increase in government functions. After considering the existing level of development and the demand for land likely to be required for administrative use, an area of 30 hectares has been earmarked towards the north eastern side of the Master Plan Area. It is also proposed that all government land under administrative use should be reorganised and planned in a proper manner so that an integrated administrative structure is attained. Besides, it is proposed that all District level offices, new administrative units be set up in the proposed administrative area.

Traffic and Transportation

Shillong has witnessed remarkable progress in all fronts but the road network has practically remained stagnant over the years. Limited road link between different activities and urban settlement, non uniform road way width, poor geometric of road intersection and absence of adequate pedestrian facilities, present a dismal picture of the traffic system.

With each passing day traffic conditions in Shillong are becoming increasingly hazardous. This also has given rise to certain vexing problems like increased journey time due to increased traffic density coupled with inadequate road capacity and traffic bottlenecks at various market junctions. The problem is further aggravated due to the mixing up of local and long distance traffic mainly on NH 40, which connect Shillong to Guwahati and NH 44. In the absence of aerial by-pass the G. S. Road is functioning as a major link for Tripura, Mizoram and Manipur and large volume of passenger and goods movement is taking place through Shillong city

In order to tackle the problem of traffic and transportation in Shillong, the Master Plan has laid down strategies like:

a) Improvement of Road Junctions and Intersections: Road junctions and intersections have been recognised as a major source creating traffic problems. After taking due cognizance of land and other physical constraints, steps should immediately be taken to improve the road junctions and intersections.

b) Widening of existing roads: The scope of roads widening does not seem to be an appropriate solution on major aerial roads, subject to availability of land, widening schemes should be undertaken to achieve the desired space standards.

c) Construction of Parking places: Parking has been considered as an integral part of overall traffic requirements. Growth on commercial activities and increase in vehicle ownership have resulted in increased parking demand especially in the central area of Shillong. The peak parking demand at several places being far excess of the parking capacity. Therefore, adequate steps need to be taken to provide parking facilities.

Shillong Municipal Board

The Shillong Municipal Board was constituted in 1910

under the Bengal Municipal Act, 1884. After independence, the functions and the powers of the Municipality were regulated by the Assam Municipal Act, 1956 which was subsequently adopted by the Meghalaya and known as the Meghalaya Municipal Act 1973. Shillong Municipal Board is at present without an Elected Board and is managed by the Nominated Board. Besides the Chairman and the chief Executive Officer there are 10 more members representing various Municipal Wards. The total number of Municipal Ward is 27. There has been no elected Municipal Board since 1973 and the last election of the Shillong Municipal Board was held in 1966.

The total area within the Municipal limit is 10.36 sq.km. which has remained unchanged. However, the operation of Municipal Board has increased considerably as all the vacant land within the Municipal area has been built up. The main functions of the Shillong Municipal Board uptill now has been to provide civic amenities like roads, footpaths, drains, street lighting, conservancy services, distribution and management of water supply etc. It does not provide education, health facilities and other services as offered by major Municipal Board / Corporations in the country. Even the above services are not provided to the desired level for want of funds and trained man-power. Therefore, it is urgently felt for setting up a civic body having jurisdiction over the entire Master Plan area of 174 sq. km. The present Municipal Board's boundary is limited to only 10.36 sq. km. Even at present due to the absence of Municipal Board and the Town Committees in other units of Urban Agglomeration, the level of the civic servies are not satisfactory, inspite of the fact that Government Department have extended such facilities and also maintaining them with nominal contribution from the localities. The cost of maintenance of water supply has been increasing and the time has come when the government cannot carry on with maintenance works. There is, thus, a need for a civic body which can take on such functions and maintain the services.

Since the District Council , the Syiems, Rangbah Shnong are involved in the civic affairs in the State, there is duplication and overlapping of functions. The proposed civic body (Municipal Corporation), must have representatives from the above institutions to make it more effective. Otherwise, there will not be any co-ordination and level of civic services may not improve.

Management

There are many agencies and local institutions which are responsible for providing civic amenities or are involved in this process directly or indirectly. In addition, there are Government Department and agencies like Public Works, the Public Health Engineering, the Urban Affairs, the Meghalaya Urban Development Authority, the Meghalaya Urban Development Agency which implement various schemes and programmes of the state governments.

Meghalaya Urban Development Authority is mainly responsible for enforcement and implementation of master plan. Meghalaya Urban Development Agency has been set up to implement the poverty alleviation scheme through the local Municipal Boards, Public Works Department executes all the schemes pertaining to roads and buildings, Public Health Engineering Department's task is to implement water supply and sewerage schemes. The Urban Affairs Department has been implementing environmental improvement of urban slums schemes and providing civic infrastructure including construction of parking lots. Meghalaya State Electricity Board has implemented street lighting schemes with funds released by Urban Affairs Department and Municipal Board.

It is apparent from the above, that within the same city atleast seven agencies of the Government are operating and implementing various development programmes. Most of them do not know the programmes of other agency. The result is un-coordinated development of infrastructure facilities. There is therefore a need to coordinate the activities of the various agencies in the field and also assign functions clearly to each of them. The Meghalaya Urban Development Authority is an umbrella body and expected to take on these functions, as all schemes have to be implemented within the framework of Master Plan and Zonal Plans. If that were so, the above department and agencies have to be represented in the Aurthority. At present there is no representative of the agencies except the Municipal Board and the Cantonment. It may be necessary to make amendments in the Meghalaya Town and Country Planning Act, 1973 so that the Government agencies including Syiemship and District Council are represented and contribute in the development process of the city.

Suggestions

Due to growth in size and complexity of town and changing inter-relationship of the structure of commercial activities, numerous problems arise. Such problems suggest that some form of rational plan should be used to project a logical growth of population and urban services. As the haphazard character of the growth pattern is the result of poor development decisions, we have identified some of the major problems faced by city of Shillong and some suggestions for making it comfortable, balanced and beautiful have been proposed.

(i) De-centralization and planned shifting of selected public and semi-public establishment, transport terminus and creation of parallel business and marketing centres in the newly created area should be considered as urgent useful steps in relieving the congestion and improving the conditions of life within the centralised localities.

(ii) Road widening should be taken up in the major roads of the city and along certain problem – prone segment such as those roads between Mawkhar and Bara Bazar and Mawprem - Bara Bazar. However, smooth circulation of traffic cannot be achieved unless parking spaces are generated at vintage locations especially in Bara Bazar, Polic Bazar, Garikhana and along G. S. Road. Creation of adequate space to accommodate parking needs and terminals for private buses and trucks in Bara Bazar to keep the existing road totally available for moving traffic is also suggested.

(iii)R unning of National Highway No. 44 through the heart of the city leads to congestion and obstacles in the smooth flow of traffic particularly in central localities. One of the remedies shall be the immediate construction of a bye-pass road for the traffic for Jaintia Hills, Cachar district and Tripura.

(iv) Integrated drainage and sewage system should be implemented in the urban complex to minimise ground water transport of pollutants to water bodies. Besides level of pollutants in the water course should be monitored regularly.

(v) Meghalaya being surplus in power should take the initiative in having a properly designed distribution system for Shillong to give better service to its consumers and at the same time earn revenue to improve the financial position of the board.

(vi) De-centralization of schools and colleges can be advised to avoid tremendous traffic congestion along main roads.

(vii) Narrow approach roads to various localities present problems in the pedestrian movement. It is a common sight to see buildings abutting against road and discharging waste over them. Invariably these badly damaged roads are having small craters over them. Regulation in this direction along with improvement in drains is suggested.

(viii) Besides it has been suggested that for effective planning of the city, Municipality must be extended in its limited jurisdiction (which at present is confined only to Shillong) to all adjoining towns forming Shillong Agglomeration.

It is also suggested that any development plan should incorporate the ever changing factors controlling the dynamic growth. Since planning is a continuous process, the development plan should be reviewed after every five years. Besides effective measures to be taken up by government agencies, public participation under certain circumstances is a must to solve with the intricate problem of human relationships consequent on concentrated urban living.

Shillong emerged as a British enclave of European Ward in the Khasi tribal heartland mainly as Cantonment, hill resort and administrative centre. While its immediate hinterland continues to be governed by tribal customary laws, the new station required skilled manpower which was not locally available. Thus, migrants came to Shillong from various destinations turning it into a multi-ethnic melting pot. With the passing of time, Shillong expanded beyond its original limits necessitating various urban amenities such as housing, marketing, hospitals, schools, roads and so on. The successive Governments of Assam and Meghalaya tried to provide the city with various urban amenties, but in the absence of law (which is under the control of traditional tribal authority) no urban development could be meaningfully undertaken. Thus, the provisions of Master Plan for Shillong may appear impressive on paper, but they may remain unachieved. Meanwhile, population of Shillong will go on increasing adding to the woe of the residents.

6

CONCLUSION

The trends of urbanization in India indicate urban growth at selected areas (mostly those which had some beginning in the past). Masses of people are migrating to such areas either from the small towns or the rural areas. Migration is also found in stages as observed by Bose (Ashish Bose 1974). The large cities are expanding in terms of population and areas, whereas the rural areas still accommodate a very large proportion of population; but there is a great disparity as defined by the economic indicators. In the west, however, such redistribution of population and econonmic activities in the big cities is associated with lesser and lesser population on the farms. Therefore, the observation is that the cities grow and rural areas loose their population. It is also observed in India, that not only is the population being concentrated in larger cities, but the problem of rural poverty and under-development is simply flowing into the urban areas. The large cities are thus growing in the number of poor people rather than through economic activities (Desai, 1968). Conditions of living in the urban areas are also not as they should be. The cities are overcrowded, congested and lack of housing and various amenities. (Balsara. 1970).

The majority of the people are still in the rural areas, and it is quite natural that the thinking in India should be oriented to the rural areas since the aim of any planning will be to benefit the maximum number of people with the available resources. While thinking of industrialization as a tool for economic development, it would be quite natural to think of avoiding large-scale concentration of economic activities particularly of industries. However, the experience is that industry is largely concentrated at a few locations mostly in the big cities, but still as observed by Peach (Peach, 1968), industrialization and urbanization, so stably married in the West, are often divorced in India. Peach points out that the match-makers of policy have aimed at industrialization without urbanization and have achieved urbanization without industrialization. It could even therefore be said that, in a way, India is experiencing slower urbanization and rapid urban growth trends in the last six to seven decades. But the question is not that simple. It is necessary to examine the economic development and urban growth patterns simultaneously and more critically. To quote Peach again, the economic growth in India after the gaining of independence is spectacular , but it has not been the cause of urbanization or urban growth. Though industrialization has created large employment, it has not been sufficient to alter the occupational structure of the country's work force. The proportion of population living in urban areas has somewhat increased, but the proportion working outside the primary sector has not increased.

It will be seen from the above that the occupation pattern at the all India level has hardly changed. Urban growth and urbanization is thus not as much a product of industrialization and occupational changes, as of population shift from the poverty- stricken hinterland to the big cities, with which people have been identifying their hopes for the future. Not only industrial development and business, but also the Five-Year Plans and the various planning programmes such as housing and social amenities sponsored by the Government have generally been found to benefit the rich rather than the weaker sections of the society.

On the whole, the urbanization pattern and the development trends benefit a few and are tilted in favour of those who can control the resource allocation and generation. The rich and the new rich have quietly amassed wealth through land speculation, luxury housing, black market operations and tax evasion (Bose, 1974). The growing disparity in society (Dandekar and Rath, 1971; Bardhan,

1974) and the gap between the economic growth and social amenities put a strain on the lower strata of the society. The pattern of industrial and urban development in such circumstances is described by many as over-urbanization (UNESCO, 1957), bourgeois industrial and urban pattern. As Bose (Bose, 1974) points out, the problems of urbanization and urban development have not, however, received adequate attention. The Five-Year Plans leave it as a subject for local administration, though national issues are also involved. Bose also expresses that the municipal administrations are not in a position to deal with these problems as they are not strong enough to carry out necessary functions and are also centres of political pressurization, corruption and administrative inefficiency and are weak in resources (Ashish Bose, 1974). The issues involved in urbanization and urban development are really complex and are not just the matters of investment in urban infrastructure or just regulating the flow of migration to cities. The whole subject has to be understood in the wider context of the economic growth and the social and the political change.

While considering the problems of economic growth and urbanization, it has to be noted that by and large the Indian society is still a rural one. However, a process of rapid urbanization is already before us. On one side, we have the metropolitanisation trends in the form of the growth of big cities and urban agglomerations, and on the other, we have large rural tracts with vast and growing rural population living on traditional farming with age-old beliefs and living patterns. A sort of dual society, thus, continues to exist with problems on both sides, and there are also the conflicts and clashes on the course to be followed for development and modernization of society as a whole. The western course of industrial and urban growth in the recent past is also before India and the other developing countries, but neither can they get a long gestation period for transforming their societies into modern-urban societies, nor can they pass on their burden to the other countries like the colonial powers (M.S. Gore, 1973). These countries are, thus, caught up in the trends of unplanned, imbalanced urban growth and many of them have adopted planned approach to their developmental problems to avoid or correct the inconsistencies, imbalances and inequalities. Some countries are ahead and others are watching them, but by and large all are sailing in the same boat with their eyes towards the developed countries and their sophisticated modern-urban societies.

Because of the high proportion of rural population and yet inadequate food production, arguments are always made that, countries like India should concentrate on agriculture, rural development and cottage industries rather than on the western type of industrial-urban development. This argument comes from two quarters. The western experts, especially the economists, think that industrialized countries should continue to produce industrial goods and agricultural countries produce agricultural produce for economic reasons, and others, essentially from Gandhian and Sarvodaya groups, who are opposed to the big cities because of their association with the colonial rule. Thinkers like Jawaharlal Nehru, tried to take both viewpoints together, thus, trying to develop basic industries and improvement in agriculture. This thinking and the policies that followed, have led to a peculiar pattern of growth in Inidia.

To briefly state again, the colonial rule in India laid the foundations of a particular development pattern in which urban and industrial growth took the typical shape in a capitalistic pattern. But a full-fledged capitalistic pattern was also not allowed to develop as industrialization was severely restricted and the urban- based administration was oriented to the needs of the colonial rule. The impetus to urbanization in India came from (1) centralization and modernization of the administration, and (2) opening up of the foreign trade. The resulting pattern was quite different from the pre-industrial society. Different types of urban areas such as railway towns, hill stations, revenue administration centres, civil and military cantonments, new trading and manufacturing centres etc., were created by manipulating the forces of growth. The municipal bodies were also developed as subservient bodies. Different new occupations and classes of people were created.

The British rule had another effect, which carried important implications for urbanization and urban growth trends related to modernization and social change. The new administrative system, educational system, transport and communication systems and industrial growth (whatever limited nature it had, and the restrictions on it) all had influence on the social organization here. In a way, the colonial rule was also responsible for the rise of political and social reformers coming forward and trying to introduce changes in the society.

With the increase of urban centres in the North East India, scholars got attracted to study the growth of these emerging new towns. Some aspects of urban phenomena which we have tried in this study have been studied by various scholars, but no one has attempted to study the urban social structure of Shillong. Though definition of a town differs from country to country and from time to time within a country., definition of town given by the Indian census 2001 has been used in this study. Thus, demographically, Shillong has been classified as Class I town by the census of India (2001).

Shillong today is an integral part of the urban system of North-east region, which is in nexus with metropolis of Calcutta urban system developed around the port. The growth of the city can be attributed to the peculiar location of the city in a predominantly tribal and hill areas with limited sedentary agricultural practices and inadequate transport linkages within and surrounding region. It is located at about 5000 meters above mean sea level, and its location provides relief for exasperated administrators, the planters and other fortune seekers from the oppressive climate and often hostile social life of the plains. No doubt, the British colonial rulers had reasons to call it as the "Scotland of the East". The objective of the present study was to understand the urban social process conceptually and empirically. Apart from reviewing the relevant literature and identifying the nuances of colonial heritage in Shillong, we tried to uncover the quality of modernity found in the city empirically from two select localities.

The influx of the various ethnic groups in Shillong has had both positive and negative effects. From the positive side, the influx has brought about development in the field of education, business and other activities. It brought about a sense of unity and integrity among the locals. It makes the local people to work and strive harder, and to have a healthy competition. This would definitely raise their standard of living. The Khasis are believed to have had a healthy interchange of ideas and cultural values through the past years. Whatever problem that has come about is not because of the influx and their intermingle, but because of the failure of one's determination, breakdown of the family, norms, mores and values in the society. Anti-social elements are present everywhere, and they exist in whatever existing population.

On the negative side, the scene is different. The influx of the 'outsiders' (all the other ethnic groups, not belonging to the Khasi community) have caused nothing but antagonism. Many Khasis believe that they would be better off without the intrusion. The various social evils like drugs, alcoholism etc. have all been brought about by other neighbouring groups, for example from Manipur, or Nagaland. Though there is no hard evidence for this claim, but one thing that is sure is that it never existed in the indegeneous society. Also, due to the influx, unemployment is rampant, admission into colleges has become more difficult, more drop-outs, and to get easy money, outsiders lure the local youths into all kinds of anti-social activities like drug peddling and the like. Lastly, the failure of the state law machinery and religious institutions to check on this have also been thought off.

The various ethnic groups in Shillong are being treated equally amidst ethnic diversities. Their relationship in day to day life is being maintained in a cordial manner. What is expected from this relationship is a friendly environment. For a 'Khasi', he would prefer safety, security and peace with the other members, and this happens likewise too for other ethnic groups.

Shillong city from time to time organises sports events, shows, tournaments, competitions etc. All are expected to be given a fair chance in such events. For example, the

Laitumkhrah Sports Social and Cultural Club, which opens up door for people of all ethnic groups to participate. In social gatherings like a 'get-together' of every locality, or during Christmas, *pujas*, *diwali* or marriage ceremonies we find members from different ethnic groups participating. Similarly, during cultural programmes like the *Shad Nongkrem* (Khasi religious dance) at Smit for example, Khasi folk would always invite friends from other communities to attend. They too would always co-operate. Cultural programmes that are sometimes organized, give a fair chance to all the groups to participate.

The cultural relationship that exists in Shillong is the kind of relationship that Simpson and Yinger calls pluralism. The pluralism that is reflected in Shillong is when both the majority, and the minority value their distinct cultural identity, while seeking at the same time economic and political unity. The minority group members cherish their cultural heritage and do not wish to loose it, and the dominant group is willing to accept cultural variations. In Shillong, groups live and let live; they respect one another's differences, but no one tries to change anyone else or make them conform to a conception of 'correct' culture or life-style, adding to lusture to the ethnic mozaic of the city of Shillong.

Shillong, is not only of diverse ethnic group, but also of diverse religious beliefs. There are 'Christians', who include the Presbyterians, the Catholics, the Baptists, the Seven-Day Adventist, and other non-denominational faiths; the Muslims, the Hindus, the Buddhists, the Sikhs, the indigenous religions, which do not come into the limelight much. Every religion is expected to be treated at equal level. What is amazing in Shillong is that, there has been an adoption of each other's religion amidst the differences in ethnic identities, i.e., a Khasi becoming a Hindu, and a Hindu becoming a Christian. Further-more, this adoption does not deprive them from any sense of achievement. Majority say that he or she is identified and accepted from both sides, both as a Khasi and a Hindu, or as a Hindu and a Christian at the same time. But then, we cannot ignore that both sides have their share of negligence. One would say, a Hindu becoming a Christian should be thrown out of the group, or for a Khasi becoming a Hindu likewise. This kind of development has agonised the youth, as reflected in ethnic identity or communal conflicts.

The post-independence period envisaged a total re-organization in the power structure of Shillong. The all important British bureaucrats had gone away and the provisions of the Sixth Schedule of the Indian Constitution ensured certain legal guarantees to the scheduled tribes. The new bureaucrats turned out to be the plainsmen, more familiar but less acceptable. The presence of new rulers, the national political parties – was hardly noteworthy in the city. There was emerging a rudiment of more aggressive tribal middle class. The newly introduced development and welfare schemes needed personnel and skills at all levels. The small administration was enlarged. A better infrastructure – roadways, buses, posts and telegraph, banks, schools - was introduced in large numbers. In such a situation, Shillong turned into a place of opportunities. All these resulted in the swelling of the urban population (Sinha A. C. 1993).

In Shillong, apart from Shillong Municipality, the traditional authority of the *Durbar Shnong* (local council) has the most important function and role to play. The functions of the *Durbar Shnong* is to look into the problems and affairs of the people irrespective of ethnic diversities, and to create a peaceful relationship amongst them. Slight tension that may creep up is being dealt with in a very proper and smooth way. Anti-social elements are being dealt with fairly. Whether it is related to drugs, alcoholism or extortion of money, persons found indulging in such activities are being severely punished.

From the foregoing analysis of the chapters, the following broad findings can be highlighted;

(i) Shillong was established mainly for administrative purposes. Throughout the history of its evolution, it has ascribed a certain degree of specialisation to its service and functions which seems to continue in future as well.

(ii) The overall position of Shillong Urban Agglomeration within the total urban population of the state is overwhelming. Whereas the total urban population of the State constituted less than one-fifth of the total population of Meghalaya, a disproportionately large share of the urban population of the state resides in Shillong, which accounts for about 72 percent of the total urban population of the State.

(iii) The city has undergone a radical change from a hill resort to a multifunctional service city, catering to a host of administrative and other service functions not only for the State but for the entire north-east region.

(iv) Shillong has also developed as a commercial centre, stretching its hinterland to the neighbouring States of South Assam, Mizoram, Tripura etc., as an important transit point in trade and commerce. With location of various types of market, and offices of the various financial and business houses, the town has emerged as an important commercial centre operating as an outlet for products of this region to various other states of the north-east and vice-versa. Shillong has been attracting people as an important tourist center and health resort.

(v) The distribution of housing in space produces its social differentiation and specifies the urban landscape. The distribution of residential location follows the general laws of distribution of products and services, and, consequently, brings about regrouping according to the social capacity and affiliation of the citizens, that is to say according to their income, education levels, ethnic composition etc., resulting in social stratification in the urban system. Thus, distinct ethnic groups by their concentration in a particular locality have acquired particular characteristics.

(vi) On the basis of economic conditions of the inhabitants, age of buildings, amenities and degree of congestion, the residential area of Shillong is classified into four categories, namely, high class, middle class, low class and slums. It is interesting to note that these residential areas have followed some definite trends with the expansion of the town, which incorporated most of the fringe areas as intermediate zones, while new fringe area developed recently will serve as periphery.

(vii) Of the total area of 17400 hectare in Shillong, 31.58 percent is developed, 9.04 percent underdeveloped and 4.62 percent under urban agriculture. The total area under administrative use is 117.93 hectare or 0.68 percent of the total plan area. There has been tremendous pressure on land and land value has increased manifold within the municipal area, during the last decade. Further, due to non-availability of buildable land within the municipal area, the development of residence has sprawlled along the major arteries of the capital.

(viii) The upcoming satellite urban centres like Madanyrting, Nongthymmai, Mawlai, Nongmynsong have higher pace of intensification in comparison to Shillong Municipal area. This indicates the steady development of fringe settlement, than the core of the city.

(ix) Traditional law pertaining to the land, forest are for preservation of the tribal right against the encroachment by non-tribals. By definition, the process of urbanization cannot be ethnic specific. So urban development will mean emergenc of multi-ethnic, social mozaic.

(x) The participation by its citizens in Shillong suggests a political culture which has a split image. It is predominantly a Khasi tribal town in which display of Khasi cultural traits is pronounced. At the same time the tribesmen appear to be reluctant to participate and share with the non-tribals the formal political structures, associations and institutions.

Shillong is mainly administrative and residential in its functional character and this character has been maintained basically. Its commercial and educational functions have developed more or less in proportion with the increase in the population, whereas the defense function has assumed much greater significance during the last few decades. Shillong is also the centre for employment, a collecting and marketing point for products of the surrounding areas, a distribution centre for incoming goods, a centre for providing higher education and specialised health services for the whole supporting area providing entertainment and cultural contact facilities, a centre dissemination of information through various communication media, and above all, a centralizing point for the local as well as sub-regional thoughts and feelings. It is a place of refuge to surrounding people and their ideas as well as a reservoir of new ideas.

The most significant point in respect of the influence of the city is its functional linkages with Brahmaputra valley on the north and the Barak valley and the adjoining states of Mizoram, Manipur and Tripura on the south, south-west through Silchar, the largest town in that valley. Its interaction with the plain areas in terms of people, goods and ideas is an important as the city's interaction with its own hinterland in the surrounding areas.

If modernity is defined purely in descriptive terms such as high rate of urbanization, predominance of non-agricultural source of income, interpersonal relation not based on kinship and ethnicity in terms of profession and other group interest, then Shillong perhaps is not very modern. The large majority of the population of Shillong are the Khasis and their personal relationship is governed mainly by ethnicity and cultural identity. Electoral politics in Shillong is not free from this consideration. The Church and Khasi traditional *Durbar* play a very important role in Shillong among the Khasis. Regarding the source of income, majority of its citizens in Shillong prefer government jobs, as both large and small scale industries being almost non-existent in Shillong. A small section of citizens are managed to reckoned their livelihood in trade and commerce like whole-sellers and other consumer goods. It is true that high rise of RCC buildings are replacing the Assam type houses very fast.

The claim of modernity and modernization in Shillong has already created visible problems, that is the evils of so called modernity. The Shillong town is not a planned town; it grew and developed on its own. The roads of Shillong were not made for maintaining and adjusting so many vehicular traffic. Shillong is perhaps one of those State Capitals in the country, where National Highway passes through the middle of the town. As a result, it has given rise to traffic jams, congestion and so on. It has been observed that many people have become rich by way of getting contracts from the Government, wholesale dealership, setting of medical nursing homes etc. This section of people may claim to be modern on the basis of their income and occupation. Another group of people, who are in government service, lead a life closer to the above segment of the population.

It is true that like any other big cities in India, luxury hotels including restaurants, cinema halls and up-to-date fashion shops are coming up but these cater only a small set of urban population, like big businessman, beaureaucrats and politician. But this can not be treated as a sign of modernity. Shillong cannot be regarded as a modern town in terms of education. Various colleges in and around Shillong including North Eastern Hill University impart education mainly in traditional subjects in arts and science. There is no professional and technical institution worth their names like medical, dental, engineering, and other professional institutions in Shillong.

Undoubtedly, these, "non-tribal towns in the tribal settings" (such as Shillong) were not established with active tribal participation. The non-tribal institutions such as public buildings, corporations, schools, libraries, clubs etc. are considered as alien, strangers and unwelcomed industries. As such distant forces created the cities and provided them with some of the historical landmarks, the same paternalistic attitudes continue to be relevant. In case one asks "whom do the city belong" and "who governs it", the answers are not obvious. This city do not belong to the common citizens, in the sense that they control the urban affairs; governs its establishments; plan for its development and feel proud of being its citizens. It is still, by and large, the formal state bureaucracy, which governs the city. But the days are not far when acute urban problems, such as housing, transportation, slum-clearance, environmental pollution, vagrancy, intoxication, urban crime against property, ethnic conflicts etc. will go beyond reasonable limits. These will be the heritage arising out of urbanization without industrialization.

"The dominant ethnic groups of this city appear to have an ambivalent attitude to the city in which they live. It seems that in the ultimate analysis, they identify themselves less with the city and more with the particular tribal traditions, in which urban experience is a new phenomena. They are masters of the affairs on the exclusively ethnic platforms, but their own city, which is decidedly ethnic plus provide an arena beyond their past experience. The civic problems are complex and demand specific care. The common impression one gets that even knowledgeable and concerned citizens do not like to take all the possible advantages of the urban living, but in their own involvement in the civic affairs they follow the '*haat*' ethic" (Sinha, A. C. 1993).

The constitutional provisions of safeguarding the tribal customary laws come on the way while implementing many of the above decisions taken at the formal level with a view to solving at least some of the urban problems. There is even impressive Master Plans for future development of Shillong. They are excellent example of good intentions, but will and commitment to improve the quality of life appears to be missing. Thus, the city of Shillong may be condemned to remain a tribal enclave with modern trappings and citizens may be subjected to the ills of a chaotic town.

BIBLIOGRAPHY

Alam, S. M., 1965, *Hyderabad-Secunderabad Twin Cities – A Study in Urban Geography,* Allied Publishers Pvt. Ltd.

Ali, Ahmed, 1983, *The pattern of distribution of languages in North Eastern Region.*

Allan Schnaiberg, 1970, "Measuring Modernism: Theoretical and Empirical Explorations", *American Journal of Sociology,* Vol. 76.

Anderson, Nels, 1959, *The Urban Community: A World Perspective,* London : Routledge and Kegan Paul.

Anderson Nels, 1960, *Urban Community.* London: Routedge and Kegan Paul.

Baer, G., 1966, *Population and Society in the Arab East,* London (transl. H. Szoke).

Balsara J. F., 1970, *Pattern of Social Life in Metropolitan Areas,* Delhi: Planning Commission India.

Bardan, P. K., 1974, "Some Aspects of Inequality" in : Ashish Bose and others (ed.), *Population in India's Development 1947-2000,* Vikash Publishing House, New Delhi.

Bareh, Hamlet, 1987, *The History and Culture of the Khasi People.* Shillong

Blumenfield Hons, 1967, *Modern Metropolis in Cities.* Penguin.

Bose, Ashish, 1959, The Process of Urbanization in India: 1901 – 1951, Unpublished Ph. D. Thesis, Delhi University.

Bose, Ashish, 1974, 'Six Decades of Urbanization in India: 1901-1961', in : M. S. A. Rao (ed.), *Urban sociology in India,* Orient Longman, New Delhi.

Bose, Ashish, 1976, *Bibliography on urbanization in India: 1947-1976,* Tata McGraw-Hill, New Delhi.

Bose, Ashish, 1978, *India's urbanization, 1901-2001,* Tata McGraw-Hill, New Delhi.

Bose, Ashish, 1990, *Urbanisation in India.* Tata McGraw-Hill, New Delhi.

Bose N. K, 1968, *Calcutta, a Social Survey.* Lalvani Publishing House, Bombay.

Bose, Nirmal Kumar 1965, Calcutta: 'A Premature Metropolis', *Scientific American,* September.

Breese Gerald, 1969, *Urbanisation in Newly Developing Countries-Readings on Urbanism and Urbanisation.* Englewood Cliffs: Prentice Hall.

Brush, John E. 1962 'The Morphology of Indian Cities', in : R. Turner (ed.), *India's Urban Future,* Berkeley: University of California Press.

Burgess, E. W. (ed.) 1925, *The Urban Community,* Chicago : University of Chicago Press.

Burgess, E. W, 1923, "Growth of the city", Proceedings of *American Sociological Society,* 18.

Chakraborty, N., 1990, Urban Poverty and the Poor in Shillong: Explorations inform content and Structure. Ph. D. Thesis., Department of Geography, North Eastern Hill Unversity, Shillong.

Chaudhury, J. N. 1978, *The Khasi Canvas,* Chapala, Shillong

Census of India – 2001. Series – 18, Meghalaya, part – 2.

Dandekar, V. M. and Rath, N., 1971, *Poverty in India,* Bombay, Indian School of Political Economy.

Das, N. C. 1986, 'Urbanisation Trends in North East India with special reference to Assam' in : B. Dutta Ray (ed). *The Pattern and Problems of Population in North East India,* Uppal Publishing House, New Delhi.

Davis, Kingsley, 1962, 'Urbanization in India: Past and Future' in : Roy Turner (ed.), *India's Urban Future,* California :University of California Press.

Davis, Kinsgsely, 1955, "The Origin and Growth of Urbanization in the World", *American Journal of Sociology.*

Desai P. B., 1968, "Economy of Indian Cities", *Journal of Public Administration.* July-Sept.

Dickinson, R. E., 1951, *The West European City,* London.

Dimock, Edward, C. and Inden, Robert, B. 1970, 'The city in pre-British Bengal, according to the Mangala Kanyas', in : Richard L. Park (ed.), *Urban Bengal,* Michigan : Michigan State University, Asian Studies Centre.

Dkhar, C. I. 1981, 'Shillong: Origin and Development: 1846-1947' M. Phil Dissertation, North Eastern Hill University, Shillong.

D'Souza, V. S. 1971, 'Urban Studies: A Trend Report' in : *A Survey of Research in Sociology and Social Anthropology,* Vol. I, Popular Prakashan, Bombay

D'Souza, Victor S., 1968, *Social Structure of a Planned City :Chandigarh,* Orient Longman Ltd., New Delhi.

D'Souza, Victor S. 1974, 'Urban Studies' in : M. N. Srinivas, M. S. A. Rao and A. M. Shaw (eds.), *A Survey of Research in Sociology and Anthropology,* Vol. I, Popular Prakashan, Bombay.

Dube, S. M. 1971, *Urbanisation in Tribal Areas in the North East India,* U. G. C. Project Report, Department of Sociology, Dibrugarh University, Dibrugarh

Duncan, M. 1963, In K. S. R., Gowda, (1972) *Urban and Regional Planning.* Mysore University of Mysore.

Dutta Roy, B. and Agnihotri, S. K., 1993, *Dynamics of a Tribal Society,* Uppal Publishing House, New Delhi.

Edwards Michael, 1961, *History of India,* London: Thames and Hudson.

Gandhi, Raj, 1983, 'Social structure of urban India: Constinuities and Change', in : Giriraj Gupta (ed), *Urban India,* Vikas Publishing House, Delhi.

Ganguly, J. B., 1995, *Urbanization and Development in North-East India.* Deep & Deep Publications, New Delhi.

Geddes, Patric, 1949, *Cities in Evolution, London:* Williams Norgate.

Ghosh, A., 1973, *The City in Early Historical India,* Simla: Indian Institute of Advanced Study.

Ghurye, G. S., 1962, *Cities and Civilisation,* Popular Prakashan Bombay.

Gibbs, J. P. (Ed.), 1966, *Urban Research Methods,* New Delhi: Affiliated East-West Press Private Ltd.

Gibbs, J. P. (ed.), 1961, *Urban Research Methods*, New York.

Ginsburg, N. 1967, "The city and Modernization", in : *Modernization: The Dynamics of Growth, a V. O. C. Series*, Madras: Higginbothams.

Gist, Noel P. 1957, 'The Ecology of Bangalore, India: An East-West Comparison', *Social Forces*, Vol. 35

Gore M. S, 1973, *Some Aspects of Social Development*. Bombay: T. I. S. S.

Goswami, B. B. 1978, *Cultural Profile of Shillong*, Anthropological Survey of India, Calcutta.

Gurdon, P. R. T. 1975, *The Khasis*, Cosmo Publications, New Delhi.

Hagget, P., 1983, *Geography: A modern Synthesis*, Harper and Row, New York.

Hambly, Gavin, 1968, *Cities of Mughal India: Delhi, Agra and Fatehpur Sikri*, London : Eleck.

Harris, C. D. and Ullman, E. L. 1945, "The nature of Cities"; *Annals of the American Academy of Political and Social Science.*

Hatt, Paul K. and Albert J. Reiss Jr. 1957, *Cities and Society*, Illinois: Free Press.

Hozelitz, B. F., 1955, 'Generative and Parasitic Cities', *Economic Development and Cultural Change*, Vol.3.

Hussain, I., 1993, *Shillong: British Enclave to Tribal city*, in Sinha A. C. (et.al).

Hoyt, H., 1939, *The Structure and Growth of Residential Neighbourhoods in American Cities*, Washington.

Inkeles, Alex 1969, Making Men Modern: "On the cause and consequences of individual change in six developing countries", *American Journal of Sociology*, Vol. 75.

Inkeles, Alex and Smit, David H. 1974, Becoming Modern. Cambridge Mass: Harvard University Press.

Johnson cf. C. S., 1943, *Patterns of Negro Segregation*, New York.

Joseph R. Gusfield, 1967, "Tradition and Modernity: Misplaced Polarities in the study of social change", *American Journal of Sociology*, Vol. 72.

Kapardekar, H. D. 1986, *Social Aspects of Urban Development*, Popular Prakashan, Bombay.

King, Anthony, D., 1976, *Colonial Urban Development: Culture, Social Power and Environment*, London, Routledge and Keagan Paul.

Lampard, E. E., 1965, 'Historical Aspects of Urbanization' in : P. M. Hauser and C. P. Schnore (ed), The *Study of Urbanization*, New York.

Learner. D. 1964, *The Passing of Traditional Society: Modernizing the Middle East*. Free Press, New York.

Lotha, Chenio, 1997, A Sociological Study of a Naga Town. M. Phil dissertation, Department of Sociology, North Eastern Hill University, Shillong.

Louis Irving Horowitz, 1966, *Three worlds of Development*, New York: Oxford University Press.

Mahapatra, A. C. 1989, *Growth of Urban Population in North East India: Policy Implications: 1951-1981*, Deptt. of Geography, North Eastern Hill University, Shillong.

Majumdar, D. N. 1987, 'Prospects of Urbanisation in North East India' in : B. Dutta Ray (ed) *North East India 2000 A.D.*, Deep & Deep Publications, New Delhi.

Majumdar, D. N., 1960, *Social Contours of an Industrial City: Social Survey of Kanpur, 1954-56*, Asia Publishing House: Bombay.

Mann, Peter H., 1965, *An Approach to Urban Sociology*, London: Routeledge and Kegan Paul.

Marx, K., and Engels, F., 1950, *Selected Writings*, Vol. I, International Publishing House, Moscow.

Mayer, P. and I. Mayer, 1974, *Townsmen and Tribesmen*, Oxford University Press, Cape Town.

Mitchell, J. C., 1966, 'Theoretical Orientations of African Urban Studies', *Anthropology of Complex Societies*, London: Tavistock.

Mitra, A. 1970, *Capital City*, Thompson Press, New Delhi.

Mukherjee, R. K., 1940, *Man and His Habitation: A Study in Social Ecology*, London: Longmans, Green and Co.

Mukerjee, Radhakamal 1961, 'Ways of Dwelling in the Communities of India', in : George A. Theodorson (ed.) *Studies in Human Ecology*, Illinois: Row Peterson and Co.

Murphy, R., 1972, "City and Countryside as Ideological Issues: India and China", Comparative *Studies in Society and History,* 14(3), June.

Mumford, L. 1961, *The City in History: its Origin, its Transformation and its Prospects,* London.

Mumford, L. 1966, *The Culture of Cities,* Harcourt Brace Jovanovich, New York.

Nair, K. S., 1978, *Ethnicity and Urbanization,* Ajanta Publication, New Delhi.

Naqvi, Hameeda Khatoon, 1971, 'Urbanization and Muslim Rulers of India', *Islam and Modern Age,* 2 (3).

Nongbri, W. L. Mebada, 1988, Ethnic Groups in Laitumkhrah: Shillong. M Phil dissertation, Department of Sociology, North Eastern Hill University, Shillong.

Pahl, R. E. (Ed.) 1968, *Readings in Urban Sociology,* London: Pergamon Press.

Pakem, B. (ed) 1984, *Shillong: 1971-1981,* Research India Publications, Calcutta

Pandey, Rajendra, 1988, *Modernisation and Social Change.* Criterion Publications, New Delhi.

Park, R. 1952, *Human Communities,* Free Press, New York.

Park, Robert E. (1952), *The city for Human Ecology*: II, New York: The Free Press.

Peach G. C. K, 1968, "Urbanisation in India" in R. P. Beckinsale and J. M. Houston (Ed.), *Urbanisation and its Problems.* Oxford: Basil Blackwell.

Quinn A. James, 1967, *Urban Sociology,* Eurasia Publishing House, New Delhi.

Rao, M. S. A., 1970, *Urbanization and Social Change: A Study of rural Community on a metropolitan Fringe,* Orient Longman: New Delhi.

Rao, M. S. A. 1974 (ed), *Urban Sociology in India,* Orient Longman, New Delhi.

Rao, V. L. S. P. and Ramachandran, R., 1974, *A Report on the Socio-Economic Survey of Vijayawada city,* Department of Human Geography, Delhi School of Economics (Mimeographed).

Redfield, R. 1941, *The Folk Culture of Yucatan*, University of Chicago Press.

Redfield, R. and M. B. Singer., 1954, 'The Cultural Role of Cities', *Economic Development and Cultural Change*, Vol., 3, No. 1.

Reimer, S., 1952, *The Modern City*, New York.

Reiss, A. J. (ed.), 1964, *Louis Wirth on cities and Social Life*, Chicago University publication.

Reissman, L. 1964, *The Urban Process: Cities in Industrial Societies*, New York, The Free Press.

Ross, E. A., 1938, *Principles of Sociology*, New York.

R. Ramachandra, 1989, *Urbanization and urban system in India*, Oxford University Press., New Delhi.

Rustow, D. A. & Ward, R. E. (Eds) 1964, *Political Modernization in Japan and Turkey*. Princeton University Press, New Jersey.

Rymbai, R. T., 1979, *The Khasi Heritage*. Shillong.

Sarlkwal, R. C., 1978, *Sociology of a Growing Town*, Ajanta Publication, New Delhi.

Saberwal, Satish., 1978, 'Indian Urbanism: A Socio-Historical perspective', in Satish Saberwal (ed), *Process and Institution in Urban India, Sociological Studies*, Vikas Publishing House, New Delhi.

Saberwal, Satish., 1978, *Shillong Centenary* Celebrations Souvenir, Shillong, 1970.

Saberwal, Satish., 1978, *Shillong Master Plan, 1991-2011*, Directorate of Urban Affairs, Shillong, Meghalaya.

Shullai, L. G. 1980, *Delightful Shillong*, Shillong.

Sjoberg, Gideon, 1959, 'Cities in Developing and Industrial Societies', in Hauser and Schnore (eds.), *The Study of Urbanization*, John Wiley and Sons, Inc., New York.

Sjoberg, Gideon 1960, *The Pre-industrial City: Past and Present*, New York: The Free Press.

Simmel, G., 1950, *The Metropolic and Mental Life*. Free Press, New York.

Singh, J. P. 1980, *Urban Land-Use Planning in Hill Areas: A Case Study of Shillong*, Inter-India, New Delhi.

Sinha, A. C. (ed), 1993, *Hill Cities of Eastern Himalayas*. Indus Publishing Company. New Delhi.

Sovani, N. V. 1966, *Urbanization and Urban India*, Asia Publishing House.

Taneja, K. L., 1973, 'Morphology of Residential Areas in Indian Cities', in R. L. Singh (ed.), Urban *Geography in Developing Countries*, Varanasi.

Tisdale, H., 1942, "The Process of Urbanization" *Social Forces*.

Toennies, F., 1987, *Community and Society*, New York: Harpercollins.

Turner, Roy, 1962, *India's Urban Future*, Berkeley, University of California Press.

Ullman E., 1967, "Theory of Location of Cities" in M. H. Meyer and F. Clyde Kohn, Readings in *Urban Geography*. Allahabad, Central Book Depot.

UNESCO, 1957, "Urbanisation in Asia and the Far East", Proceedings of a seminar at Bangkok. Calcutta. UNESCO Research Centre.

Weber, M, 1958, *The City, New York*: The Free Press.

Weiner, Myron, 1967, *Modernization: The Dynamics of Growth*. Higginbothoms Ltd., Madras.

Weiner M, 1970, *Urbanisation and Political Protest, (Open University – social science course)* London: Macmillan Press.

Wirth, L., 1938, 'Urbanism as a way of life', *American Journal of Sociology*, XLIV.

Wirth, L., 1964, *On Cities and Social Life*, Chicago: The University of Chicago Press.

Wirth, L., 1980, 'Urbanization as a way of Life' in *Urban life* by Gmelch, G. and W. P. Zenner (eds), St. Martin's Press, New York.

Wirth, L., 1980, *Cities and Social Life*. St. Martin's Press. New York.

Yadav Sheo, Kumar, 1986, *Residential and Social Structure: A study in urban social geography*, Inter-India publications, New Delhi.

Yazaki, T, 1963, *The Japanese City*, Tokyo.

Young, Pauline V., 1966, *Scientific Social Surveys and Research*. Prentice-Hall of India, New Delhi.

Index

D

E

M